I0020972

CLOUD DATA WAREHOUSING

VOLUME II: IMPLEMENTING DATA WAREHOUSE, LAKEHOUSE, MESH, AND FABRIC

DR. BARRY DEVLIN

Technics Publications

Published by:

115 Linda Vista, Sedona, Arizona USA
https://www.TechnicsPub.com

Edited by Jamie Hoberman
Cover design by Lorena Molinari

All rights reserved. No part of this book may be reproduced or transmitted in any form or by any means, electronic or mechanical, including photocopying, recording or by any information storage and retrieval system, without written permission from the publisher, except for brief quotations in a review.

The author and publisher have taken care in the preparation of this book, but make no expressed or implied warranty of any kind and assume no responsibility for errors or omissions. No liability is assumed for incidental or consequential damages in connection with or arising out of the use of the information or programs contained herein.

All trade and product names are trademarks, registered trademarks, or service marks of their respective companies, and are the property of their respective holders and should be treated as such.

First Printing 2024
Copyright © 2024 by Barry Devlin

ISBN, print ed.	9781634623964
ISBN, Kindle ed.	9781634623971
ISBN, PDF ed.	9781634623995

*To Dear Friends, Colleagues, and Clients
over Four Decades of Data Warehousing*

*Without you, this book would
never have been written*

*Special thanks to my good friends, Dan Graham, Thomas
Frisendal, James Serra, and Dave Wells, who reviewed the
first draft. Your input has improved the book immeasurably.*

*Gratitude also to my publisher, Steve Hoberman, who did
so much to get this book quickly and elegantly to press,
and to Lorena Molinari for her stunning cover art.*

CONTENTS

Chapter 1

Introducing Volume II

Rows and flows of angel hair
And ice cream castles in the air
And feather canyons everywhere
I've looked at clouds that way.

Both Sides Now, Joni Mitchell

Joni Mitchell's lyrical 1968 evocation of the mysteries and magic of clouds offers a wonderful metaphor for all the possibilities that we in IT pin on the concept of "the cloud" and to cloud data warehousing in particular. And in this two-part series, I explore these topics not just from "both sides now" but from all sides, as well as past, present, and future.

My goal is to provide help and guidance to those trying to understand and implement cloud data warehousing. The audience is the managers and architects—perhaps new to data warehousing—who make the high-level decisions about their enterprise's overall approach. This is not a deep technical dive into the minutiae of cloud technologies. The goal is to help designers avoid the many pitfalls inherent in the current public discourse. There are many overlapping and contradictory definitions and terminology being offered by proponents of each model of cloud data warehousing.

Whereas the focus of Volume I was on describing the architectural foundations of **cloud data warehousing**, in Volume II we turn our attention to implementation issues and dive deeper into the **architectural design patterns**, both foundational—data warehouse classic, logical data warehouse, and data lake classic—and emergent—data lakehouse, data fabric, and data mesh.

But first, I want to clarify again what I mean by **data warehousing** and cloud data warehousing in the context of this series. The first and fundamental purpose of data warehousing is *to deliver consistent, integrated, timely, quality, useful, and usable data primarily to business users.* This allows the broadest possible view of the various solutions offered and gives a clear set of criteria against which to judge them. This helps avoid consideration of solutions whose only purpose is to format or visualize a single, existing set of data for business use.

Not unexpectedly, I use the phrase *cloud data warehousing* to mean exactly the same delivery services as above, but in the cloud, as well as hybrid and multi-cloud.

The next section offers a brief reprise of Volume I and recaps some of the key definitions, as well as much of the foundational thinking of this series.

If you have just finished reading Volume I, feel free to skip ahead to the following section, *Volume II*, which introduces the contents of this volume.

CLOUD DATA WAREHOUSING: VOLUME I

Volume I begins with a review of the history of data warehousing, exploring the breadth of thinking included in the concept and noting its varied (although sometimes conflicting) terminology. Together, these factors explain the longevity and success of data warehousing. How many times has it been declared dead by its detractors? Nonetheless, it remains as vibrant as ever.

Next up, we explore the purpose and principles of data warehousing, seen through the lens of multiple decades of experience. It is vital that these principles and their purpose are understood when considering migration to the cloud or, indeed, any major reworking or expansion of the technological foundation of an existing warehouse. This discussion leads to a conceptual architecture for data warehousing. We see that this conceptual level of architecture remains exactly the same, whether implemented on-premises or in the cloud.

Following that is an overview of a comprehensive, REAL[1] logical architecture for all forms of cloud data warehousing. Both this and the prior conceptual level are based first on the thinking in *Business unIntelligence* (Devlin, 2013) and subsequently expanded over the intervening decade.

This level of architecture is largely agnostic to where the solution is delivered, whether on-premises, cloud, or hybrid. The architecture also allows comparison of various competing vendor products. We describe the original logical architecture and then explore some key aspects where cloud data warehousing drives a change in perspective.

The next topic is the future of data warehousing, especially in the cloud. First up are the ethical and societal challenges of artificial intelligence (AI) and how they must be addressed. That is followed by a deeper dive into data storage and databases as technology evolves. Following this, the demanding topic of context and the meaning of data is addressed.

Finally, we examine how traditional data warehousing solutions can be migrated to cloud data warehousing and how emerging cloud-based systems can evolve. Ideally, such migrations avoid reworking everything that has been

---

[1] REAL = Realistic, Extensible, Actionable, and Labile. See also Volume I, Chapter 4, "Fleshing out the function."

previously, successfully achieved. We explore this from the perspective of three different, practical starting points, using the key concept of architectural design patterns (ADPs). Most implementers of cloud data warehousing will start from some mix of these starting points and ADPs, but the lessons will be equally applicable to all, irrespective of the exact nature of the journey they are undertaking.

Volume I thus sets the scene for a deeper dive into the six architectural design patterns listed earlier and should be read before this current volume.

VOLUME II OVERVIEW

The main theme of this volume is implementation. Chapter 2 begins our journey by reaffirming the definition of an **architectural design pattern (ADP)**. An ADP is a reusable solution describing the software design of inputs, data flows, functions, and outputs that solve a specific business need. It provides an agreed set of terminology and includes an illustration of data flows and functional components, as well as basic infrastructure requirements and constraints.

We dive in to take a closer look at the three foundational ADPs—data warehouse classic (on-premises and cloud-native), data lake classic, and logical data warehouse. Volume I offered short definitions and the context of their evolution.

Here, these definitions are expanded and, more importantly, we provide the enhanced logical architectural illustrations that represent each ADP. This allows a clear distinction and detailed comparisons to be drawn between the three patterns, right down to the level of technological solutions. These three pictures form the basis for exploring the emergent ADPs in Chapters 4-7.

But first, we must ask: Why do we need these new patterns? Their proponents like to list the problems of the existing data warehouse and lake solutions. We summarize these toward the end of Chapter 2 but propose they may be better used as a good basis for evaluating where the emergent pattern solution you choose may work or not, particularly in terms of nonfunctional requirements.

Chapter 3 returns to the land of architecture for one last visit. Our aim is to explore the path from information (and data) in a warehousing solution to the decisions and actions that businesspeople require. This path is neither wide nor direct in any of the foundational ADPs. The emerging ADPs—lakehouse, fabric, and mesh—also address this issue with only limited and varying degrees of success. However, as AI and machine learning (ML) encroach ever further into daily, personal, and corporate decision making, the topics of knowledge and meaning demand far closer architectural attention than they have previously received.

Chapter 4 begins our analysis of the emergent patterns, starting with the data lakehouse. Bearing a close resemblance to the data warehouse classic (cloud-native) ADP, the data lakehouse provides an obvious pathway and destination for anyone moving from a largely centralized on-premises data warehouse and/or data lake to the cloud. Given this resemblance, exploring the data lakehouse ADP provides the ideal opportunity to discover how cloud data storage and population technology and methods differ from those familiar on-premises.

Chapter 5 unravels the data fabric ADP. Data fabric has evolved principally from the logical data warehouse. Its starting point is thus highly decentralized and the challenges it addresses relate strongly to the management of data in such a distributed environment. Here, *management* includes the creation of and access to information stored in disparate and distributed locations. Key to this is **active metadata** that is gathered and kept current through the use of AI and other modern techniques. It is used in real time for all aspects of data management. The relationship of such active metadata to context-setting information (CSI), introduced in Volume I, may be obvious, but will be clarified here.

Finally, we untangle the data mesh ADP in Chapter 6. It is a unique approach to cloud data warehousing and is very different from all the previously mentioned patterns. Excluding centralized storage and organizational structures from the outset, data mesh applies a number of concepts that are largely unfamiliar in mainstream data warehousing. These include domain-driven design, data as a product, and micro-services-based implementation, all embedded within an automated, distributed governance mantle. Straying far from traditional data warehousing implementation approaches, data mesh offers some challenge to depict it in the same enhanced logical architecture used for all the other patterns.

Chapter 7 ties together the threads of the preceding chapters. It compares and contrasts the concepts of lakehouse, fabric, mesh, and cloud data warehouse at a sufficiently high level to allow architects, systems designers, and the businesspeople they support to broadly understand the distinctions between the different patterns. We can see why some consultants and vendors may confuse or misuse different patterns in marketing literature. This allows us to distinguish between the reality and the hype in many cases. And we offer guidance on which pattern may be most appropriate in your particular circumstances.

TAKEAWAYS

- *Data warehousing,* as defined here, covers the many approaches widely used to provide data and information to decision makers of all levels. The purpose of data warehousing is to help decision makers understand what is happening in the business (and the world in which it operates), why, and what to do about it, now and in the future. The fundamental driver of data warehousing is the delivery of consistent, integrated, timely, quality, useful, and usable data.

- The main goal of Volume II is to move from architectural to implementation considerations. Such considerations for and comparisons between different approaches to data warehousing are best described through well-defined architectural design patterns (ADPs).

- As AI plays an increasing role in decision making, defining the architectural relationship between data/information, knowledge, and meaning, as well as mapping a path from information to decisions and actions will become a vital aspect of implementing cloud data warehousing solutions. Such thinking is still vestigial but should ideally be incorporated into the design of the emergent ADPs.

- An ADP is a reusable solution describing the software design of inputs, data flows, functions, and outputs that solve a specific business need. It provides an agreed set of terminology and includes an illustration of data flows and functional components, as well as basic infrastructure requirements and constraints.

- Three foundational ADPs are identified: data warehouse classic (DWC) both on-premises (DWC/op) and cloud-native (DWC/cn), logical data warehouse (LDW), and data lake classic (DLC).

- The three emergent ADPs are data lakehouse and data fabric—evolutions of the DWC and LDW ADPs respectively—and data mesh—a completely novel approach.

- Choosing between these solutions demands a deep understanding not just of the patterns themselves but an ability to map their strengths and weaknesses to your starting point and desired destination on your journey to the cloud.

Chapter 2

Foundational architectural design patterns

Architecture, as anything else in life, is evolutionary. Ideas evolve; they don't come from outer space and crash into the drawing board.

Bjarke Ingels

Into our cozy world of warehouses and lakes, three new ideas—data lakehouse, data fabric, and data mesh—have crashed, not from outer space, but as outgrowths from our existing solutions. Our first task, therefore, is to construct a common understanding of these solutions. To do this, we will use the language of architectural design patterns.

An **architectural design pattern (ADP)** is a reusable solution describing the software design of inputs, data flows, functions, and outputs that solve a business need. It provides an agreed set of terminology and an illustration of the solution, as well as basic infrastructure requirements and constraints. It must offer sufficient detail for a solution architect to envisage how it could be implemented, but at a high enough level that its picture fits on a single—possibly large—sheet of paper. It must be implementable with current or near-term available technology, without being tied to a particular product. The picture should contain no product names.

Figure 2.1 shows the REAL logical on-premises architecture[2]. It is the base for the three foundational ADPs described here.

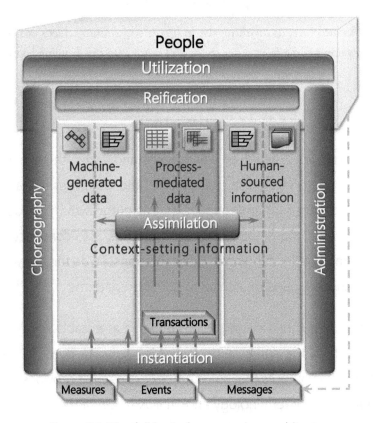

Figure 2.1: The full logical on-premises architecture

---

[2] REAL = Realistic, Extensible, Actionable, Labile. See Volume I, chapter 4.

Figure 2.2 shows the full cloud logical architecture, on which the three emergent ADPs are based. The only difference between the two logical architectures is in the structure of the central information pillars, reflecting the evolution of distributed data storage available in the cloud environment[3].

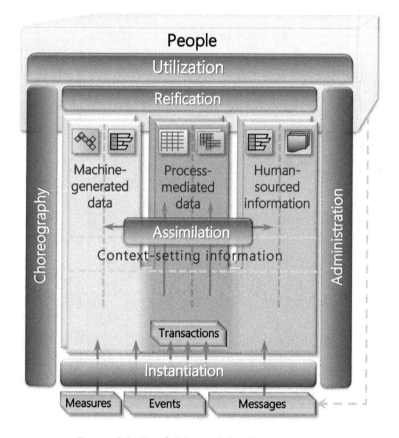

Figure 2.2: The full logical cloud architecture

---

[3] Further details of these differences can be found in *"Introducing Information Pillars"* in Volume I, chapter 4.

Recent rapid advances in generative AI may drive some re-work of the pillars in both pictures. This remains to be done.

The foundational, generic architectural design pattern for traditional solutions is shown in *Figure 2.3*.

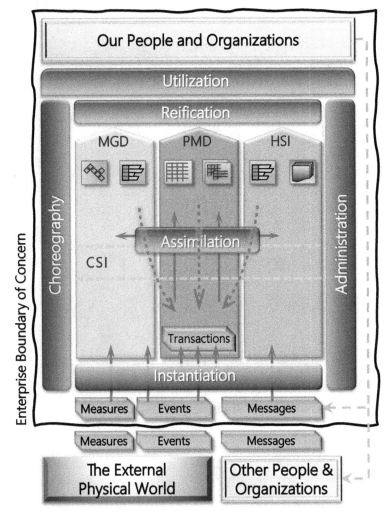

Figure 2.3: Generic foundational on-premises ADP

Building on the full logical on-premises architecture (*Figure 2.1*), this ADP depicts further architectural and organizational considerations that are important in discussing the similarities and differences between the three foundational data warehousing patterns: data warehouse classic (DWC), logical data warehouse (LDW), and data lake classic (DLC).

Note first the wavy black line annotated **"Enterprise Boundary of Concern (EBoC)"**. This is the boundary within which the designers and providers of data warehousing solutions have full responsibility. It is important for a number of reasons. First, it reminds us that the primary concern of any solution developer must be to support *our own* people and organizations in their decision making and action taking. We are also shown that these same people are the source of much of the data and information that constitutes the solution. Their activities are the ultimate source of many of the events, measures, and messages that drive the business. This was self-evident in the past, when (internal) operational systems drove most or all business activity, but it has been somewhat neglected as an increasing proportion of the business is driven by external events, measures, and messages.

Second, the EBoC emphasizes the responsibility of solution deliverers for the function and data/information within its boundary, even though some of it may reside physically beyond the enterprise. An example, previously noted, is that human-sourced information (HSI[4]) originating from social media sites may well be used in the enterprise to categorize and classify customers. However, for many reasons—legal, contractual, cost, etc.—this HSI is unlikely to be physically stored within the enterprise (or in cloud storage rented by the enterprise). Rather, it is accessed as needed from its sources. Nonetheless, any data warehousing solution must accept responsibility for the quality, security, and other characteristics of this information when used internally.

Finally, we must keep in mind that this boundary will evolve—perhaps rapidly and significantly—as the business reinvents itself in response to market pressure. At such times, executive focus may be intense, with significant implications for information ownership and governance.

Unlike in the early days of data warehousing, the role of the external world must be recognized. *Figure 2.3* explicitly shows that events, measures, and messages arrive at the EBoC from the external physical world and from other people and organizations, as well as those that travel in the opposite direction, such as the reports that our people provide to external regulatory people and organizations.

---

[4] See Volume I, chapter 4 for definitions of the data/information domains, HSI, PMD, and MGD.

Note that the data/information pillars are redrawn as upward pointing arrows. This emphasizes that the *primary* flow of data/information in data warehousing is upward, toward our people and organizations. This has always been the emphasis of data warehousing. Almost every warehousing diagram ever drawn shows only *unidirectional* data flows from the sources to the consumers of information, so they may derive insights from it in decision making and action taking.

However, *Figure 2.3* also highlights a set of **reverse flows** in the center of the data/information space. All data warehousing solutions, beyond the simplest reporting systems, contain some reverse data flows. Novice implementers may be taken by surprise by this, having only seen the above unidirectional thinking. The needs for reverse flows are many and varied. They have become ubiquitous in modern data warehousing systems. They range from relatively simple feedback loops— for example, in budget planning, forecasting, and tracking— to the needs of modern analytical and machine learning systems for complex management of models and training data. Reverse flows *must* be considered in the detailed ADPs.

We can now briefly explore the three foundational ADP pictures—Data Warehouse Classic (DWC), Logical Data Warehouse (LDW), and Data Lake Classic (DLC)—based on the generic view shown in *Figure 2.3*. These patterns are well understood in database management communities. Our purpose here is mainly to prepare for the comparisons of the Data Lakehouse, Data Fabric, and Data Mesh ADPs among themselves and with the foundational ADPs shown later.

DATA WAREHOUSE CLASSIC ADP

The **data warehouse classic** pattern was defined in Volume I as providing correct and consistent, well-modeled, schema-on-write, relevant, and usable (each *as far as possible*) information in support of business analysis and decision-making needs in a cross-business manner. A DWC may be structured as a hub-and-spoke pattern consisting of an enterprise data warehouse (EDW) and dependent data marts, as a dimensional / star-schema pattern, or some combination of both.

Although there is minimal difference between the two logical architectures above, technology drives important implementation changes. This leads to two flavors of this ADP, based on technology used (rather than physical location):

- **DWC/op:** implemented with technologies traditionally used **on premises,** based on finite servers or server clusters, using "conventional" relational database technologies from vendors such as IBM, Oracle, or Teradata.

- **DWC/cn:** built on **cloud-native** technology, which is loosely defined as automatically elastic and scalable, leveraging object storage, with clearly separate compute and storage, and multi-cluster compute.

Data Warehouse Classic/op ADP

Figure 2.4 shows the first foundational architectural design pattern: the DWC/op.

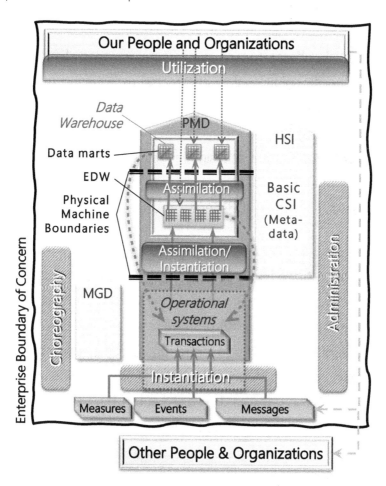

Figure 2.4: ADP: Data Warehouse Classic / On premises

In contrast to the generic ADP shown in the previous figure, it's pretty sparse—very understandable, given its limited scope and advanced years!

First note that it is focused on internally sourced process-mediated data (PMD) from traditional operational systems, shown here as the green dotted-outline box. Machine-generated data (MGD) and human-sourced information (HSI) are essentially absent from an architectural viewpoint. If included in a specific solution, they are treated as if they were PMD, leading to over-governance of such data as if they were legally binding business transactions. Metadata is included in the DWC/op pattern as a sidebar. It's shown in HSI because that is what it is in architectural terms, but it is often treated solely as something IT defines and uses.

Reification is absent and access to data (shown by the dotted, open-tipped, blue arrows) via utilization is restricted to separate, individual data marts in the warehouse, and occasional access to the enterprise data warehouse (EDW). The choreography and administration process components (shown cross-hatched) are vestigial. Utilization, often in the form of BI tools, is well developed and is the path by which data/information is provided to internal users and organizations. Instantiation exists primarily in the operational systems that are the sources of almost all the data in the system. Characterizing operational systems as instantiation may feel uncomfortable at first sight. However, recognizing that they generate business transactions from messages and, to a lesser extent, from events and measures, allows us to see that there is a strong architectural equivalence between transactions that originate in traditional data entry systems and those that arrive via website data entry by customers. Irrespective of their source, such transactions require the highest level of data governance.

At the heart of the DWC is the data warehouse, shown in *Figure 2.4* in its hub-and-spoke form. A combination of assimilation and instantiation—in the form of ETL/ELT (Extract, Transform, Load and Extract, Load, Transform) tools or even bespoke programs and scripts—plays a key role in all aspects of populating and maintaining both the EDW layer and the data marts above it.

The complexity of design, maintenance, and operation of multiple data stores in these layers and the processing between them poses a challenge for this ADP, despite its relatively restricted data scope. Such challenges have led to many claims of the coming demise of this ADP. "The Extinction of Enterprise Data Warehousing" (Strengholt, 2020) offers a good example of this class of discussion. However, as in other similar pieces, the question of how otherwise to address the primary driver of data warehousing—providing correct and consistent, well-modeled, relevant, and usable information to decision makers—remains unanswered.

Although often neglected in vendor and other high-level depictions of this pattern, a reverse flow paths from data marts and EDW to the operational environment must be included in all but the simplest implementations. Shown in *Figure 2.4* as dashed, highlighted arrows, such reverse flows create the necessary closed-loop environment for all types of sense-and-respond behavior. Data reconciled in the EDW or derived at the data mart level as a result of historical analysis should be fed back into the operational environment to reflect any learnings and/or decisions. Although such feedback can be manually implemented, as digital transformation proceeds, more automation is required.

Heavy, double-dashed, black lines represent the common positions of physical storage boundaries that both characterize the DWC/op and add a further significant challenge: operational systems reside in one environment (optimized for read/write work), while the data warehouse resides in one or more separate read- and/or analytics-optimized environments. These physical boundaries present significant barriers to the movement of data at required speeds and volumes both in a forward direction and in reverse flows.

This has led to consideration of the possibility of combining the operational and informational worlds[5]. Such an evolution would simplify many design and implementation aspects of the DWC/op ADP—and may become more realistic as most processing moves to the cloud. The logical, REAL architecture was drawn with this possibility in mind: making no assumption of or demand for separate physical operational and informational worlds. But the goal of a single operational/informational environment using on-premises technology has remained elusive. Particularly challenging are the legacy operational applications that provide the basic business transaction function to banks, insurance, airlines, and more, that cannot easily be replaced. The persistence of such systems is a challenge not just for the evolution of this ADP; it poses a fundamental problem for the Data Mesh ADP, as we shall see in Chapter 6.

DATA WAREHOUSE CLASSIC/CN ADP

The DWC/cn ADP is built on cloud-native technology, as defined in *Data Warehouse Classic ADP*. This pattern, shown in *Figure 2.5*, is functionally identical to the DWC/op pattern (*Figure 2.4*), with all data still being sourced within the EBoC.

---

[5] See Volume I, chapter 5 for further discussion.

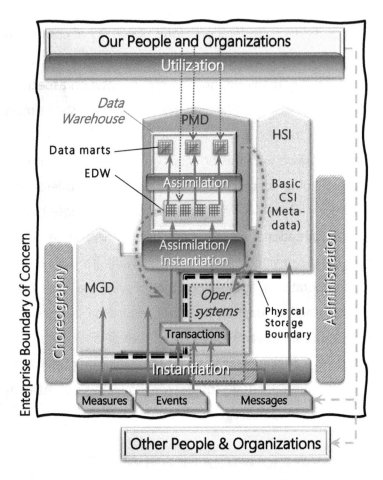

Figure 2.5: ADP: Data Warehouse Classic / Cloud native

However, moving the data warehousing function to the cloud, while (some) sources remain on premises and some also move to the cloud, adds considerable physical complexity. The awkward reshaping of the information pillars results from the mix of operational systems remaining on premises, while the rest of the environment moves to the cloud.

Logically, operational systems remain part of process-medi-ated data (PMD), as shown by the stippled blue backdrop, but are separated by a physical storage boundary—the heavy, double-dashed, black line—from the informational part of the PMD pillar. Machine-generated data (MGD) and human-sourced-information (HSI) are similarly dimmed be-cause they continue to be peripheral to the data warehouse. However, the flexibility of object storage does allow some MGD and HSI to be brought into the data warehouse.

Instantiation appears here in the true sense of the defini-tion—the process by which measures, events, and messages are represented as instances of data/information within the pillars of the enterprise information. Various measures, events, and messages arrive directly in the DWC/cn as im-plementers of this pattern build ingestion and cleansing function for data coming from cloud-based sources. In some cases, transactions—in the sense of legally binding business interactions rather than database transactions—from web apps may also be loaded. In this pattern, all this data ends up in the data warehouse via assimilation.

As in the case of the DWC/op pattern, basic CSI (metadata) is included, in this case stored in the cloud environment. Sim-ilarly, the data warehouse is largely identical to that in the DWC/op pattern, although without the need often encoun-tered in on-premises implementations to place data marts on a different platform than the EDW. People access and use data marts and the EDW individually via their apps in the utilization function as is the case in the DWC/op. Reverse data flows are similar to those in the DWC/op and may be simplified as some of the targets are also in the cloud.

This pattern is seen when software vendors, such as Snowflake, for example, implement new cloud data warehouse function. It also occurs when traditional data warehouses migrate to the cloud, as seen with Teradata VantageCloud.

As we see in Chapter 4, DWC/cn also forms a key foundation for the data lakehouse pattern.

DATA LAKE CLASSIC ADP

The **data lake classic (DLC)** pattern was defined in Volume I as offering data in raw, as-received format, usually with limited preprocessing, or with cleansing at the discretion of the user. Key characteristics include scalable data storage in any format, multiple processing models, and timely, flexible usage (schema-on-read) by users. Data governance is often limited, leading to multiple, overlapping, and inconsistent "copies" (exact or otherwise) of the same data being stored, with users left to their own devices to figure out which data to use when. *Figure 2.6* shows the next foundational architecture design pattern: the DLC in its original form.

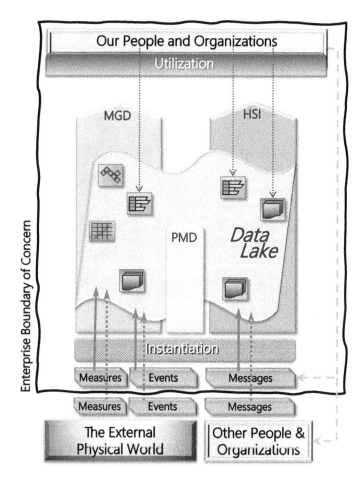

Figure 2.6: ADP: Data Lake Classic (original)

In contrast to the generic version of the ADP, it's even more sparse than the DWC/op—again, very understandable, given its limited scope. Essentially, the data lake, as originally defined, is little more than a place to land and store an unmanaged collection of data files sourced from the external physical world (the purple shaded box at bottom left). The data lake appears elegant and simple to use. The opposite is true. Without a data model and metadata, programming is needed to accomplish most tasks. In many cases, the use of point-and-click BI tools is not possible.

The data lake spans the MGD and HSI pillars. The lake doesn't distinguish between these types in any way: all data is characterized as "unstructured" or "semi-structured." PMD is also unrecognized and largely unpopulated, although some externally sourced data should be treated as such.

Of the process components, only utilization is fully developed. As in the previous pattern, access to data is to separate, individual data objects, shown by the dotted, open-tipped, blue arrows. Instantiation does, of course, exist, although it most cases, it is little more than a collection of assorted and relatively simple scripts. CSI / metadata is notable only by its complete absence, leading to a complete lack of any worthwhile data governance.

Lake + warehouse pseudo-ADP

Such a bare-bones pattern could not endure, of course. The data lake quickly came to engulf the data warehouse, driven by a range of political and financial considerations during most of the 2010s. This leads to the pseudo-pattern shown in *Figure 2.7.* Despite its busyness, this is simply a combination of two independent ADPs: DWC/op and DLC.

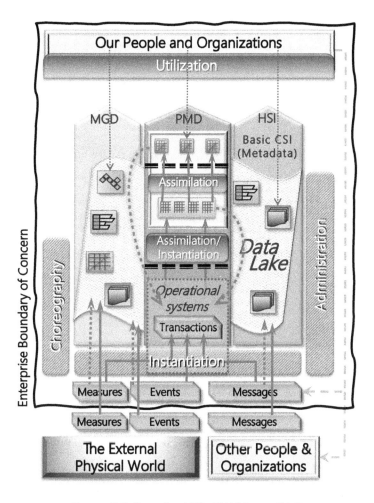

Figure 2.7: Pseudo-ADP: DWC/op + DLC

The components are as described in the previous sections. I call this a pseudo-ADP because of the complete absence of integration between its two component patterns. A data lake is built, typically in the Hadoop environment, and the data warehouse is ported from its prior platform to a relational database also in Hadoop. The operational systems remain on their original platform, and new and further assimilation/instantiation function feeds the migrated data warehouse. As before, access to data is to separate, individual data objects, shown by the dotted, open-tipped, blue arrows.

Of course, once data warehouse and lake function are placed together on the same platform, the opportunity and urge arise to share data and function between them. This would be depicted in the diagram as an expansion of the main assimilation/instantiation function beyond the bounds of the PMD pillar into the MGD and HSI pillars and further require a considerable expansion in scope of CSI beyond the basic metadata represented here.

These extensions are not illustrated here because this thinking forms the basis of the Data Lakehouse ADP. As we shall see in Chapter 4, a Lakehouse is a combination of the DWC/*cn* and DLC ADPs, both built on *cloud-native* technology. It is, of course, feasible to implement this combination of function on premises, likely building on the Hadoop ecosystem. However, the cloud-native implementation has become the go-to approach in almost all instances.

LOGICAL DATA WAREHOUSE ADP

As *Figure 2.8* shows, the logical data warehouse (LDW) is technically the most complex of all the ADPs seen so far.

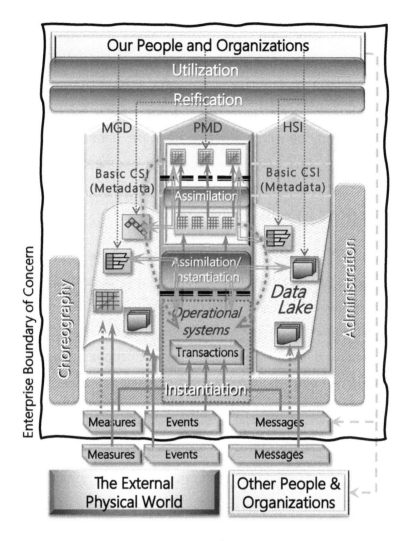

Figure 2.8: ADP: Logical Data Warehouse

It builds on the previous ADPs with the addition of a functional reification (aka data virtualization) component between the information pillars and utilization. At its most basic level, virtualization allows data from separate and, often, differently structured sources to be joined in real-time as a query is submitted by a user or application through the utilization layer. This is illustrated by the dotted, open-tipped, blue arrows accessing more than one data source. These sources may be within a data warehouse, data lake, or, indeed, any other accessible internal environment. Although not shown (for simplicity), access to live data in traditional operational systems is an important use case.

Simply joining data from disparate sources in real-time—particularly when done in addition to any prior reconciliation by the assimilation/instantiation component—gives rise to significant data quality concerns, as well as other performance and security worries[6]. Fully functional reification therefore demands underpinning physical and logical data models to ensure that data joins deliver valid and reliable results despite potential semantic and temporal inconsistency between sources. As a result, the LDW ADP requires a broader and deeper set of context-setting information (CSI), including technical metadata, than seen in the data warehouse (DWC) and data lake (DLC) patterns. *Figure 2.8* thus shows that CSI must bridge all the individual pillars.

---

[6] See Volume I, chapter 4 for further details.

This further adds to the work required of assimilation and assimilation/instantiation shown by the double, green arrows overlaying these components. These arrows represent the creation and maintenance of relationships between disparate data stores. Such relationships may be simply at the semantic level, such as relating different table, file, or field names in the stores to one another. Or it may need to go to a data content level, providing mapping tables between values in one store with those in another. A common example is where customer IDs in the EDW must be related (where legally allowed) to social media IDs in the HSI pillar.

Figure 2.8 shows the data lake seen in the two previous figures. However, early logical data warehouses were built without including such a data lake. The LDW ADP is centered on a well-defined, data warehouse classic ADP, allowing users of that warehouse to access data in other locations, irrespective of their architectural type. Today, this pattern typically includes a data lake as a key source. This follows logically from the DWC/op + DLC pseudo-pattern (*Figure 2.7*), with organizations "migrating" from a warehouse to a lake, but actually embedding an unconnected data warehouse within the data lake.

As we shall see in Chapter 5, this ADP is the foundation of the modern data fabric pattern.

PROBLEMS OF THE FOUNDATIONAL ADPs

The DWC pattern has survived and, indeed, thrived for over three decades. Both data lake classic and logical data warehouse ADPs are over a decade old with many successful implementations. Of course, there are also many failures, some spectacular, for each ADP. Nonetheless, these patterns are generally classed as successful.

Why, then, have we witnessed an explosion of new patterns over the past few years? Is it that the technological differences of the cloud environment necessitate a change? The relatively limited adaptations needed to the logical architecture suggest not. Does the cloud offer new possibilities or opportunities in decision making and action taking that require new ADPs? The analysis in Chapter 2 suggests not. Although there is some truth in asserting that current ADPs cannot meet new opportunities for ML and other advanced analytical needs, many aspects of digital transformation can be supported by the foundational ADPs. Or is it simply technologists' well-known love of "new, bright, shiny things"? ☺

The very different approaches being taken by data fabric, lakehouse, and mesh suggest that, rather than there being one or two large and obvious problems spanning all the foundational patterns, the proponents of the new ADPs are responding to specific sets of smaller, more confined issues.

These issues are, however, deeply seated in the detail of specific implementations. The list below offers readers a basis for asking: Does the new ADP I'm considering successfully address most of these problems, or has it succeeded only with some at the expense of exacerbating others?

The following list summarizes key and interrelated problems often claimed by opponents of particular foundational patterns or of a more general nature. Some may be exaggerated for effect and others offered with limited regard for the real complexity of data management. I list them not because I believe them to be true in many cases, but because they offer a basis for recalling and evaluating the nonfunctional requirements embedded in each ADP.

1. **Complexity of system design, build, and maintenance:** This has been the principal complaint raised against the DWC pattern since its inception, and it extends to the LDW. Many approaches have been employed to mitigate this problem. In the extreme, it drove—at least, in part— the emergence of the data lake.

    Unfortunately, complexity is intrinsic to the process of integrating and reconciling data/information that originates from multiple, disparate sources. Imagine integrating data models from Salesforce, Oracle Siebel CRM, and SAP Ariba Invoice Management applications.

All are written by different programming teams with different foundations. If this is the business need, such complexity is unavoidable. ADPs that promise to reduce this complexity often do so by diminishing or underestimating this business need. They tend toward siloed solutions for specific analytical needs.

2. **Challenges of semantic and enterprise data modeling:** Closely related to this integration requirement and, therefore, closely associated with the DWC, is the question of how to model the resultant data store in a way that associates disparate data with standard vocabularies and meanings of real-world business objects. An enterprise data model (EDM)—of varying degrees of sophistication and complexity—is generally accepted to be required.

   Starting from a blank sheet of paper was discovered from the earliest days to be expensive, time-consuming, and likely to fail. Generic industry models reduced these risks and have become a common approach. Defining an EDM also contributes to the complexity issues of the previous list item. ADPs that exclude some form of enterprise modeling are inherently focused on point analytical solutions rather than enterprise-level data integration.

3. **Project scale and delayed delivery:** A logical and obvious consequence of the preceding points is that development projects balloon in both cost and time. This has led to various project-staging, program-driven approaches to delivering DWC implementations. The LDW pattern partially overcomes this challenge, given its ability to deliver some needs from existing sources, although some level of reconciled data, as well as an EDM, is still required.

4. **Cross-project delivery coordination:** Any program that takes data from multiple sources faces the challenge of delivery coordination as data sources follow independent and—at best—loosely aligned upgrade and maintenance plans. Again, it is the DWC pattern that exhibits this problem most clearly.

5. **Project prioritization across organizations:** All true data warehousing patterns aim to address the needs of multiple parts of the organization, generating contention for limited resources to deliver business needs. The DLC pattern, with its limited or nonexistent structuring and preparation, is least affected by this issue. Both DWC and LDW face this challenge because of their higher levels of complexity.

6. **Multiple transformation layers:** The DWC pattern is traditionally multi-layered: operational systems feed staging areas that feed the EDW which further feed data marts. Each data layer has its own preparation and transformation function, with strong logical inter-dependencies.

   Although generally regarded as a significant improvement on the "rats' nest of stovepipes" linking individual source and target systems that preceded data warehousing, these layers have become increasingly complex. They typically contain a mix of standard function from ETL tools and bespoke code addressing unique or highly complex transformations. All this adds yet another level of design complexity.

7. **Lack of agility in maintenance or upgrade:** With such a complex data model, both logical and physical, as well as the aforementioned multiple transformation layers, even fixing minor bugs or addressing the smallest change in business needs may easily become a significant challenge. The DWC pattern suffers particularly from this issue. A class of tooling, Data Warehouse Automation, which focuses on providing a closed-loop development and maintenance environment, emerged in the 2000s, specifically aiming to address this challenge. Its sweet spot is probably at the mid-levels of data warehousing size and complexity.

8. **Centralized development teams lacking business knowledge:** With the level of design, build, and maintenance complexity described above, teams of highly skilled software engineers with deep knowledge of database optimization and ETL tools are required. In most cases, they are divorced from specific business needs and knowledge. Although this is a challenge for all large infrastructure projects, it is of particular interest in data warehousing, because BI and analytical requirements are loosely defined and highly fluid in nature. They are thus easily misunderstood or rigidly implemented by developers dissociated from the original business need.

9. **Disconnect between data providers and information users:** The previous issue adds further to the disconnect that arises from placing a large, complex data environment between the providers of the base data and the ultimate users of information derived from it.

   While often associated with the DWC and LDW patterns, this issue also affects the DLC ADP. It is particularly problematical for the lake + warehouse pseudo-ADP because of the *ad hoc* design approach often seen in these implementations.

10. **Combined operational and analytical uses:** A growing issue for all foundational ADPs is the convergence of

operational and informational/analytical usage of data. Operational use cases—simplistically, demanding record-level, read/write transactions—were traditionally separated from informational use cases—basically, needing set-oriented, read-only access. This was possible because business needs were simpler, and most technology couldn't handle both use cases at volume. Digital transformation has radically increased the business need for combined use, but the foundational ADPs are based on the physical separation of operational and informational systems.

11. **Centralization and duplication of large volumes of data:** As data volumes have grown, serious concerns have arisen around the centralization and duplication of such data. Both the DWC and DLC patterns promote such centralization, with the DWC also encouraging duplication across its multiple layers. The LDW ADP suffers to a lesser extent.

    Storage and processing expenses cannot be dismissed, despite decreasing hardware costs and the use of open-source software. However, the main concerns are the data management costs and complexity associated with this burgeoning growth of data stores, potentially containing inconsistent, duplicated, poorly managed data.

12. **Lack of data quality and consistency:** The DLC pattern suffers particularly from a lack of data quality and consistency. This problem emerges from the design decision to eliminate data preparation on load (in order to speed data delivery or offer raw, as-loaded data to users such as data scientists). While the lack of consistency that arises from this approach may not be problematical in certain use cases, the consequences of poor data quality are generally disastrous to business decision making and, indeed, to the reputation of IT.

It is this latter data quality issue that led to the emergence of the term *data swamp* and is among the largest risks of any DLC project.

Although long, this list of concerns and issues is indicative rather than comprehensive. It illustrates the range and types of problems that have been cited as rationales for the emergent ADPs that will be explored in later chapters. The earlier part of the list focuses on issues principally seen in the DWC pattern. We then encounter issues that more generally apply to multiple patterns, before finishing with the most common issue with the DLC.

Spoiler alert: it is sadly the case that none of the modern ADPs solve all of these problems. In many cases, one of the above issues is solved only to introduce or exacerbate one of the others. In some cases, the issues stem from the complexity of the real world—both in modern business needs and in the distributed nature of data. *Caveat emptor.*

There exists a further area of concern for anyone who has been involved in data warehousing over its long history. How effective is the data in warehouses and lakes in contributing to decision making and bridging to action taking? Before moving on to the emergent ADPs, we consider this important architectural question in Chapter 3.

TAKEAWAYS

- An architectural design pattern (ADP) is an agreed set of terminology with a picture encapsulating the key business needs and basic infrastructure requirements and constraints of a solution. It offers sufficient detail to envisage how it could be implemented, but at a high enough level that its picture fits on a single page.

- An ADP must be free of specific product names but rather show generic function and, only if necessary, illustrative types of technology.

- A generic, foundational ADP, based closely on the full logical data warehouse architecture, forms the starting point for drawing three distinct foundational ADPs.

- The first is the DWC, data warehouse classic. This ADP provides *as far as possible* correct and consistent, well-modeled, schema-on-write, relevant, and usable information in support of business analysis and decision-making needs in a cross-business manner. It may be a hub-and-spoke EDW with dependent data marts, a dimensional / star-schema approach, or some combination of both.

  Two flavors of DWC exist: one, DWC/op, is based on typical on-premises technology; and the other, DWC/cn, is based on cloud-native tooling.

- The DWC/op ADP focuses entirely on internally sourced process-mediated data. It shows the traditional separation of the operational environment that generates business transactions and the informational systems such as the EDW and data marts. Hard, physical machine boundaries separate these components, with that between the operational and informational environments found in all implementations. The important and often overlooked reverse flow of data from data marts and EDW to operational systems is shown. A separate, basic CSI (metadata) store is also included.

  This ADP represents all forms of traditional, on-premises data warehouses since their inception in the mid-1980s.

- The DWC/cn ADP shows the implementation of the data warehouse classic pattern on cloud-native technology. With data sources now both on premises (as previously) and in the cloud, ingestion and feedback processes become technically more complex, but in terms of business needs satisfied and functional components, this pattern is essentially the same as the DWC/op ADP.

- The data lake classic, DLC, ADP offers data in raw, as-received format, usually with limited preprocessing, or with cleansing at the discretion of the business user. Key characteristics include scalable data storage in any format, multiple processing models, and timely, flexible usage (schema-on-read) by businesspeople. The DLC pattern treats all types of data—PMD, MGD, and HSI—in the same way: raw and largely unmanaged. Given its limitations, pure DLC implementations are now rare.

- Over the past half-decade, the term *data lake* has come to mean a loose combination of DWC/op and DLC patterns that we may call a pseudo-ADP.

- The final foundational ADP is the LDW, logical data warehouse. It extends the DWC/op ADP with direct, real-time access to data in any required sources, such as operational systems, files, NoSQL stores, etc. It may be thought of as a formalized lake + warehouse pseudo-

ADP with added function for data management and virtualized data access across all the stores.

Access is mediated through an overarching logical, semantic data model describing the different data sources in a common language. It also insulates users from underlying differences in format and meaning. Data is typically accessed through SQL or SQL-based apps.

- A list of twelve putative issues with existing data warehousing solutions (based on the foundational ADPs described here) is provided. They are often used as justifications for the data lakehouse, data fabric, or data mesh patterns. However, they are best used to understand and evaluate the nonfunctional requirements inherent in any particular pattern.

It should not be assumed that the new patterns will solve all the problems as identified. At best, they are concerns that must be traded off against one another... as has always been the case in architectural definition and design.

Chapter 3

From Information to Action via Meaning

Words mean more than what is set down on paper.
It takes the human voice to infuse them
with shades of deeper meaning.

Maya Angelou

There exists a pervasive belief among proponents of BI and analytics that the provision of more information to business-people leads inevitably to better decisions. This article of faith should perhaps be questioned as we move from one generation of ADPs to the next. Could new ADPs improve the pull-through from data to decisions? And, as generative AI becomes pervasive, automating or augmenting our human decisions, do we really understand in any depth how data or information drives or influences real-world actions?

In short, is the human voice needed to infuse data with shades of deeper meaning and ethical action taking?

Numerous studies correlate the adoption of "data-driven" approaches with improved business results. A decade-old McKinsey report, "Using customer analytics to boost corporate performance" (McKinsey, 2014), states "The likelihood of generating above-average profits and marketing earnings is around twice as high for those that apply customer analytics broadly and intensively." The report, and many like it, lists many impressive correlations. However, the results often lean heavily on the self-reported and self-described *opinions* of managers about their own performance.

A more recent research report, "The New Decision Makers: Equipping Frontline Workers for Success" (Harvard Business Review, 2020), also uses a self-reporting approach. It says that "Eighty-seven percent of the 464 [responding] business executives... say their organization will be more successful when frontline workers are empowered to make important decisions in the moment." Even in its use of data to prove the value of being data driven, this study could do better.

At the other end of the hype spectrum, a plethora of studies over the past quarter century show that the penetration of BI tools remains stubbornly low. BI/analytics adoption stands at 25% to 35% of the business population and has hardly grown at all over that time (Avidon, 2023). The article's upbeat title, "BI adoption poised to break through barrier – finally," is based on the suggestion that "the combination of embedded BI, NLP and development of a data culture could result in a breakthrough." But is this really true?

We gather and manage huge and increasing quantities of data, but only a tiny percentage of it is used by a small fraction of the business. And yet, we continue to believe we can and will succeed... if only we can find the right BI and AI technology, management methodology, or some other codology[7] to make it happen!

There seems to be a mismatch between our expectations of what data/information can do for the business and what current and anticipated tools and techniques can deliver. Should we ask more of decision making and action taking than simply becoming data driven? W. Edward Deming's oft quoted "without data, you're just another person with an opinion" is good advice. But, a more recent play on it, "without an opinion, you're just another person with data" (Jones & Silberzahn, 2016) may be equally worthy of consideration.

With this in mind, let's revisit our thinking about how we proceed from data and information to decisions and action in the real world of modern business.

---

[7] Codology: *Irish informal*, the art or practice of bluffing or deception, Collins Dictionary.

THE DILEMMA OF THE DECISION MAKER

As a person[8], in both business and personal situations, how do *you* make a decision? Do you try to explore options and evaluate possible outcomes in advance? Do you excel at Microsoft Excel or BI tools, enjoying the challenge of finding, shaping, and exploring extensive data? Or do you find yourself frozen by the range of possibilities and/or the uncertainty of your predictive powers? Do you jump—at first or at last—to some preferred, gut-felt decision? Or do you try to validate or confirm that preference using data? Finally, do you act with confidence on your decision?

Of course, we all differ as people, as do the situations we deal with, but it is probably fair to say that our personal decision making spans the whole gamut of these options. However, in business and, especially, economics, decision making theorists favor **rational choice theory** or some close derivative of it and consider it to be the only correct methodology.

Dating back to the 18th century, pure rational choice theory is based on the idea that individuals make decisions based on some form of cost-benefit analysis, rationally and

---

[8] Parts of this chapter are reproduced by permission of the Insurance Data Management Association, from their Course Book, *Approaches to Data Design, Engineering, and Development* (IDMA and Devlin, 2023).

consistently applied on the basis of self-interest. The assumption is that such individual decision making will collectively produce an optimal aggregate outcome, usually named in the economic sphere as the "invisible hand." According to economist Tim Harford: "Economists are always looking for the hidden logic behind life, the way it is shaped by countless unseen rational decisions" (Harford, 2008).

The theory has been expanded over many years to include bounded rationality (by Herbert A. Simon), choice under uncertainty, subjective (or Bayesian) probability, and the absence of one perfect process for making decisions (the Vroom-Yetton model). The common theme of all these methods is their statistical and probabilistic basis. They thus depend on an extensive foundation of data to analyze, and they lead directly to the widely promoted idea of becoming data driven. However, in cases where human preferences and behavior are central, the data may be estimates, proxies, or, in the worst case, guesswork.

This sole focus on data as a basis for decision making is unfortunate and risky. Information is far more important and useful than data. But even information alone is insufficient. Why is it that people with access to the same information make different or even contradictory decisions? What value do humans add to information in the process of decision making? Such questions have been posed since the earliest days of management information systems, and one of the earliest and longest lasting answers dates to 1989.

DIKW—Data, Information, Knowledge, Wisdom

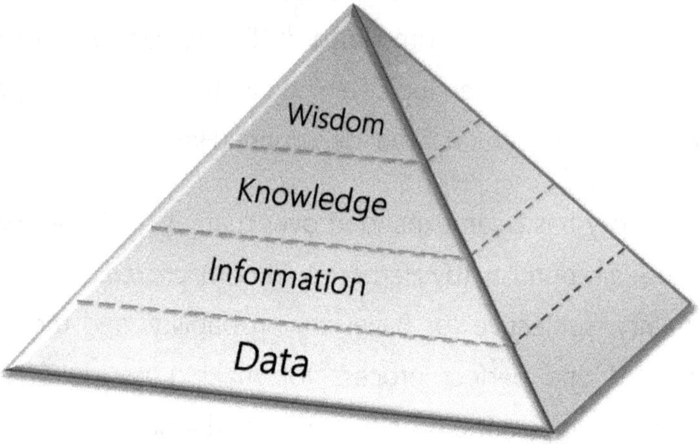

Figure 3.1: DIKW, based on Ackoff

Russell K. Ackoff, a renowned management consultant in the 1980s, defined a hierarchy with data at the base and tiers of information, understanding, and knowledge leading to wisdom at the apex (Ackoff, 1989), often drawn in the shape of a pyramid. Understanding is omitted from most representations, as shown in *Figure 3.1*—authors add or subtract terms to suit their needs—and the framework is widely known by the acronym DIKW.

Ackoff suggested—based, ironically, on gut feel, by the sound of it—that "on average about forty percent of the human mind consists of data, thirty percent information, twenty percent knowledge, ten percent understanding, and virtually no wisdom". Definitions of the terms and the relationships between them have been continuously disputed since, but the general sense expressed in the above "pretended" percentages still holds sway.

Ackoff's model is flawed in multiple ways: data is a subset of information as seen in Volume I, and thus cannot be the foundational layer shown, knowledge does not flow entirely from immediate information, and wisdom is undefined. However, the model has persisted because, if viewed from the perspective of decision making, we start the process with data in some store, derive information from it by, for example, creating some graphs, and enhance our knowledge of the problem or solution as a result. The implications of this way of thinking are that we miss the fundamental differences between data, information, and knowledge, and can be misled by the unfounded idea that wisdom has any role in mundane, business decision making.

THE MANIFEST MEANING MODEL, M³

The manifest meaning model, m³, shown in *Figure 3.2*, is an improved conceptual model of the relationships between data/information, knowledge, and meaning that I proposed a decade ago in *Business unIntelligence* (Devlin, 2013).

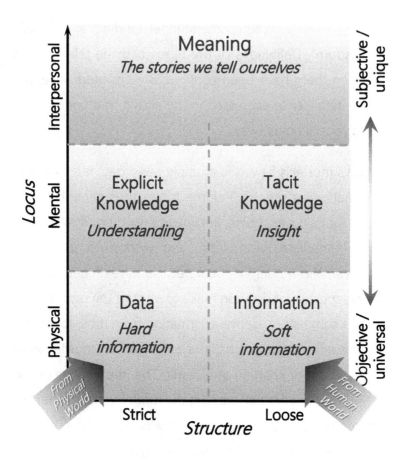

Figure 3.2: The manifest[9] meaning model, m[3]

The horizontal axis, **structure**, is one of the key characteristics that differentiates data from information[10]. This characteristic also applies to knowledge. We note, as before, that data

---

[9] Originally called the "modern meaning model".

[10] Data vs. information was explored in Volume I, chapter 3.

originates in the physical world of sensors and devices, whereas information or content is a human construct[11].

The vertical axis, **locus**, which ranges from physical, through mental, to interpersonal, shows "where" we find each concept in the real world of computers and people. On the right, we note another key characteristic. Whatever is physically instantiated—information, in this case—becomes objectified and thus (potentially) universally applicable, whereas anything in the interpersonal locus is essentially subjective and unique to the context in which it is understood and used.

Locus: data/information

Information and data occupy the lowest, physical locus of m^3. Both, as we saw previously, are forms of information, structured hard and soft, respectively. The difference between them also relates to **context**—both in creation and subsequent use. The presence or absence of **context-setting information (CSI)** distinguishes between context-rich information and context-poor data. **(Naked) data** is thus a subset of information from which context has been stripped to the maximum extent. In the simplest terms:

_____

[11] The clarity of this clear separation between data and information is being eroded by AI in its increasingly human-like ability to "interpret" and generate text, images, and video. This is beyond the scope of this book.

Information = Naked Data + Context

The qualifier *naked* is added to illuminate the word *data* on its own, which is often used to mean different things, sometimes even to stand for *information*.

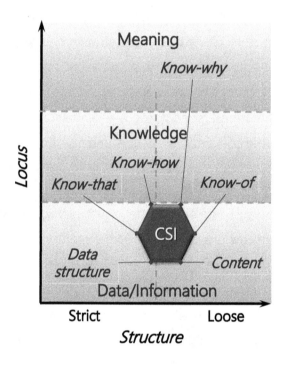

Figure 3.3: Context-setting information in m³

Figure 3.3 positions CSI within the manifest meaning model, where it is clearly part of the data/information locus. At that level, CSI performs the traditional metadata-like functions, such as data definitions, descriptions, and structure, of which it is a superset. With respect to the knowledge and meaning

loci[12], CSI addresses the various forms of **knowing** often discussed in knowledge management:

- Know-how: skill to carry out specific tasks, some of
  which is embodied in processes and procedures.

- Know-of: awareness of the existence of various types
  of knowledge and information.

- Know-that: reasoning from basic facts to more complex concepts, structural knowledge, and patterns,
  including underlying know-what, know-who, and
  know-where.

- Know-why: a deeper kind of knowledge, understanding the wider context.

Locus: knowledge

The mental locus of m^3, **knowledge**, exists *only* in the human
mind and emerges through lifelong exposure to information
in all forms and experience of the reality of cause and effect,
personal engagement, education, and more. It consists of
explicit and tacit knowledge. The difference between them is
that explicit knowledge can be easily expressed, codified, and

---

[12] *Loci* is the plural of *locus.*

shared; whereas tacit knowledge is rooted in personal experience and more difficult to express, codify, and share.

Explicit knowledge can easily be confused with information, often seen in the discipline of knowledge management, which may focus almost exclusively on managing the information representation of knowledge in the organization.

The usual example of tacit knowledge offered is how to ride a bike. However, in business decision making, tacit knowledge equates to the **insights** that an experienced person may bring to a situation. Such insights may go far beyond the explicit information that BI or analytics provides, based on data directly related to the subject matter in hand. The business expertise and, in some cases, life experience of the decision maker may well contribute to such insights. The BI dashboard may show green, but the manager—having walked the production line and noticed some oddities— knows that the sum of these tiny anomalies signals danger.

The phrase *gut feel* is sometimes used to cover some aspects of tacit knowledge. In effect, insights come from prior digested information and internal mental heuristics, informed or prompted by the current information. In the data-driven paradigm, gut feel is regularly dismissed as "unscientific" and to be rigorously avoided. This, however, is an unfortunate simplification and incorrectly assumes that valid, relevant, and reliable data is available for all decisions. Where data is sparse, unreliable, or even too complicated or extensive for human cognition[13], gut feel may well be an appropriate or even the only available approach. Gerd Gigerenzer of the Max Planck Institute for Human Development provides an insightful explanation of these processes in *Gut Feelings* (Gigerenzer, 2007). In other words, both quantitative and qualitative insights are useful. Both sources of insights can also be flawed.

In the business world, decision-making *leaders* usually excel in applying gut feel appropriately and effectively, moving between explicit and tacit knowledge, especially in relating prior and often unconscious information and context to the situation at hand:

$$\textbf{Knowledge = Information + Experience}$$
$$\textbf{(+ Gut feel)}$$

The information/data available about a current problem or opportunity—via a BI tool, for example—should be an input to a person's knowledge of a situation. However, this information is likely interpreted in the context of pre-existing knowledge that may strongly influence how the new

---

[13] Our current love affair with AI proposes that it can augment human cognition for huge data sets. However, we must bear in mind the sources of such data and the historical and other biases often embedded therein.

information is received. Where the data and gut offer contradictory signals, the decision maker must be cognizant of possible **cognitive bias**, a topic that receives considerable attention—much of it negative—in discussions about decision making. Wikipedia offers hundreds of such biases (Wikipedia, 2023), describing them as "systematic patterns of deviation from [the] norm and/or rationality in judgment."

Locus: meaning

The interpersonal locus, **meaning**, is the major interchange on the journey from information/data to action. *Meaning* replaces wisdom in DIKW because it doesn't carry the value judgment that wisdom does. It also better reflects the importance of personal relationships and social context when information is interpreted, knowledge used, and judgments reached. Most of us have observed the phenomenon. Information is interpreted differently in different situations and with diverse audiences. Judgments and conclusions change, and decisions subtly shift during meetings. The knowledge of the presenter meets that of its recipients and morphs, delicately or deeply, as the shared emotional signals massage the message to (hopefully) an agreed meaning. Or, if not, at least to expose what's needed to achieve consensus on where major issues lie. Thus:

Meaning = Knowledge + Humanity

We humans are, at heart, social animals and business is a social enterprise. Deeply understanding what information and knowledge mean, why that is so, and what are the human and societal implications almost always occurs in a social context. We all exchange information and knowledge and enjoy the ensuing debate! Therefore, understanding which decisions and actions are appropriate occurs in this locus of the model. Meaning is, in the final reckoning, the stories we tell ourselves and others about the information we gather and the knowledge we hold. As a result, decisions are seldom, if ever, fully explainable with complete rationality.

DATA—OR INFORMATION—MANAGEMENT?

m^3 offers food for thought to data management theory and practice. For a start, we may question the term *data management* in relation to what it is expected to achieve. The goal of improving basic *data* quality is too narrow to drive business value to the fullest possible extent. To rename it *information management* would be a small step in the right direction. To be truly impactful, the remit of data management must reach further to knowledge and meaning.

Of course, data managers cannot climb into the heads of businesspeople to excavate and improve their knowledge. Nor can they compete with the social and organizational inertia inherent in large or complex businesses. However, when data managers recognize the importance of all three loci and address concerns at each level, their efforts to improve data quality, however successful today, will increase business value far more than they might imagine.

Raising the sights of data management above basic data quality improvement requires getting actively involved in the full solution-design cycle. As the business first describes—in the initial stages of solution design—their requirements, what questions need answers, and the stories to be told, data managers must be intimately involved in teasing out the data and information implications of the request. They must be engaged in feeding—into the earliest design process—the nuances of the data that actually exists or that could be captured. It is they who will have to explore data lineage, address issues of data ownership, and suggest considerations of privacy or ethics.

A Single Version of the Truth or a Single Source of Truth

In the light of m^3, the traditional concept of a **single version of the truth (SVOT)**, is seen to be impossible. Truth, like beauty, is in the eye of the beholder, and exists at the meaning level of m^3. Financial concepts such as profit per customer are often defined very differently by different parts of the organization. Even fundamental entities, such as customer or order, may take on different meanings depending on context. Banks must grapple with customers who are persons as well as customers that are corporations. In any large organization, there exist multiple versions of "truth." Both business and IT must understand in what context different beliefs and stories about data/information are deemed "the truth" to ensure that alternative stories are also considered.

Another misnomer, but for different reasons, is the **single source of truth (SSOT)**. Defined as the practice of structuring data models and data stores such that every data element is mastered in only one place, this concept is valid. However, it might be more correctly called a *single source of fact.* Like single version of the truth, single source of truth challenges us to consider what exactly is stored in our databases and how they relate to one another. This is, of course, the topic of data and information modeling.

It should now be clear that being data driven alone is not really a good thing; without context, data on its own may lead its users astray. Answers emerge at every level of m^3. Some answers are simple facts, some are synthesized into knowledge or meaning influenced by possible bias. Knowledge plus an expert's bias can often be ideal for decision making. Or the bias can be wrong. Given the widespread admixing of data and information terminology, we might say that *data driven* might be better expressed as **information enlightened** (see *"Data driven or information enlightened?"*).

Transformations in M³

Perhaps as important as the layers of locus in m³ is understanding the paths between them. These transformations, shown in *Figure 3.4*, are central to the journey of business-people from information/data to action.

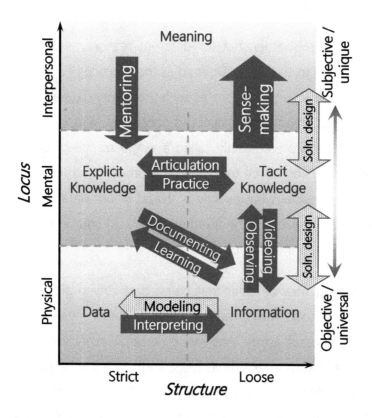

Figure 3.4: Transformations in m³

Information is transformed into data via data/information **modeling** which is then stripped of much of its context, which is then stored and managed separately. (At least in principle, as much context is today only informally documented and often mislaid). The reverse process of transforming data into information, interpreting, occurs in BI and analytics tools, the first step of which requires businesspeople to reconnect data to its separated context. As observed in Volume I, different types of data stores separate data and context to differing extents. Key:value stores contain essentially naked data, while document stores, such as MongoDB, mix data and context freely. Where context is lacking or lost, businesspeople improvise, often with predictably inconsistent results.

In decision making, explicit knowledge corresponds to an understanding of a situation, whereas tacit knowledge may be equated to insights about its underlying characteristics. Similar to the case for data and information, the processes of articulation and practice allow movement between tacit and explicit knowledge. *Figure 3.4* also shows the processes by which knowledge and information are transmuted from one to the other. The relationship between explicit knowledge and information via documentation and learning is traditionally the primary pathway. However, recent changes in the way we acquire and disseminate knowledge via video. Training videos on YouTube, for example, show a growing trend toward documenting (or attempting to document) tacit knowledge. Finally, the processes of **mentoring** and **sense-making**[14] link knowledge and meaning.

The dark blue, solid arrows discussed above relate to the on-going use of the information/knowledge/meaning by businesspeople. Also shown in *Figure 3.4* are green, stippled **solution design** arrows linking all three loci, with modeling similarly colored. These arrows relate to the design and development of information delivery solutions. Solution design is the iterative process by which business meaning and knowledge are translated into information, followed by data modeling to transform that information to data. These processes are, to a large extent, driven by IT and data management on behalf of the business, ideally involving businesspeople extensively throughout. Much of the procedural complexity of data warehousing implementation arises from the convergence of these topics.

FROM MEANING TO ACTION

Figure 3.5 below first illustrates the fact that we cannot get directly from information/data to decision making. We must traverse knowledge and meaning. As we saw, the knowledge locus is where insights are gained; where specific information of a particular situation is combined with the broader

---

[14] For further details, see *Business unIntelligence* (Devlin, 2013).

information and expertise garnered over a lifetime or career, often experienced as **intuition** and **gut feel**, coming in from left field in the diagram.

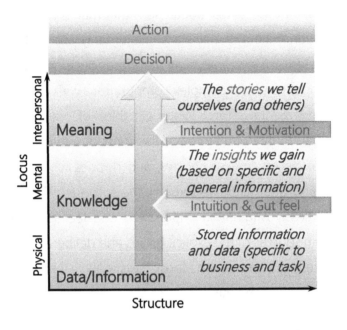

Figure 3.5: Adding Decision and Action to m³

In the meaning locus, we are influenced by our emotional states, social conventions, and especially by **intention** and **motivation**, swayed by our own and others' expectations and needs. True business leaders apply appropriate ethical and societal context when non-leaders may act for personal gain and ignore social implications. With **meaning**, we move fully from the objective world of facts and figures to a largely subjective and contextually unique view of the world. And it is from this space that decisions are made.

Economics Laureate Daniel Kahneman provides one easily accessible view of how individuals make decisions in *Thinking Fast and Slow* (Kahneman, 2011). They use some combination of System 1 (fast, pattern detection) that makes rapid, automatic judgements or decisions involuntarily and with ease, and System 2 (slow, analytical) that bases decisions on careful comparisons and complex computations with consciousness and mental effort. "When we think of ourselves," he says, "we identify with System 2, the conscious, reasoning self that has beliefs, makes choices, and decides what to think about and what to do. [However], the automatic System 1 is … effortlessly originating impressions and feelings that are the main sources of the explicit beliefs and deliberate choices of System 2." Kahneman doesn't distinguish between the knowledge and meaning loci. His focus is mainly on individuals and their use of tacit and explicit knowledge—the foundations of Systems 1 and 2, respectively. Where he does consider emotion or motivation (the meaning locus), he often frames these almost as corruptions of the fast or slow "thinking" of the book's title.

Kahneman ascribes great power to System 1, but favors System 2 as the means of blocking errors originating from fast thinking, if only we could switch to it quickly and effectively enough. He suggests that decisions made in organizations are more reliably System 2-based: "Organizations are better than individuals when it comes to avoiding [such] errors, because they naturally think more slowly and have the power to impose orderly procedures." Using the analogy that an organization is a decision-manufacturing factory, he concludes that constant quality control of decisions made is the proper way to improve decision making. However, he offers limited insight on how the social forces at play within all organizations can and do derail so many decisions.

Lights, camera, action

The distinction between decision and action—and the transition from one to the other—is often overlooked in data warehousing and business intelligence. This may be traced back to the focus on decision theory and its reliance on statistical and mathematical approaches based firmly on data. The currently popular phrase *data-driven decisions* marks the decision as the goal, although it is actually in the subsequent action where real business value is achieved. Decisions without follow-on actions are essentially pointless. Plus, the correctness or value of the decision can only be measured when action is taken.

Crossing the gap from decision to action generally requires no further analysis of data/information; it is a human-centric and organization-driven process. As we shall see later, none of the architecture design patterns (ADPs) pay attention to this part of the value chain of cloud data warehousing. In terms of comparing the various ADPs, this topic offers limited input. However, with the burgeoning growth of AI and its application to all aspects of business (and life), it becomes vital to consider the transition from meaning—and the decisions taken based on it—to action. The replacement of humans by AI in this transition is likely to have widespread and deep impact with potentially dangerous societal implications.

ADDING ARTIFICIAL INTELLIGENCE TO THE MIX

Decision making and action taking are conventionally divided into three levels, as shown in *Figure 3.6*, where the pyramidal shape suggests both a hierarchy and the volume of activity at each level.

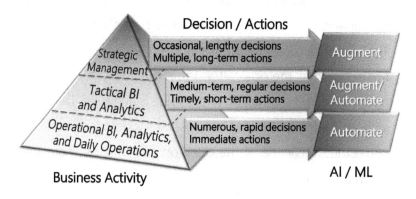

Figure 3.6: Decision/Action Levels

Traditional BI systems and less complex analytics began with and still focus principally on **tactical decisions**. Such decisions have medium term (days to months) outcomes and are made by mid-level managers, based on well-known and well-understood data/information, mostly process-mediated data (PMD). The characteristics and sources of the data used in this environment have strongly influenced data warehousing, particularly from a cross-enterprise point of view.

Decision-making support has also long aimed at aiding **strategic decisions**—although with less success than at the tactical level. Such decisions have long term (months to years) horizons and high financial impact, are made by executives, and should (ideally) be influenced by relevant information, often human-sourced information (HSI).

At the lowest level, **operational decisions** operate with a short time horizon (seconds to hours), each with mostly limited financial impact, and are made by operational managers and staff as part of keeping the business running. Automating such decisions has long been a common goal in **operational BI** or **operational analytics** systems. Such decisions are founded on basic data, often machine-generated data (MGD), increasingly coming from external sources. When operating effectively, ten thousand small operational decisions a day often add up to reduced costs and increased profits.

The flags posted on the right of *Figure 3.6* map the two opposing aspects of AI and ML to these three levels. Briefly, automation replicates and replaces human activities, while augmentation complements human activities, enabling people to do things never previously conceived[15]. The top and bottom levels clearly align with augmentation and automation, respectively. However, the mixture at the tactical decision-making level is especially worrying. That worry arises from AI's relationship to the popular concept of *data driven.*

Data driven or information enlightened?

Much of the drive to become **data driven** has its genesis in the area of operational decisions, based increasingly on externally sourced data. Carl Anderson, in his comprehensive *Creating a Data-Driven Organization* (Anderson, 2015) correctly sets the broadest scope in terms of the activities that must be addressed to enable "collecting the right data, [ensuring] that the data is trustworthy, the analysis is good, that the insights are considered in the decision, and that they drive concrete actions so the potential can be realized." Despite the nod to *insights* here, closer examination confirms that the subject matter is indeed data, metrics, A/B testing, and statistical techniques. m^3 clearly positions insights as emerging from contextualized human knowledge.

---

[15] For a deeply insightful (and very worrying) discussion of how society and business promote automation over augmentation and the likely consequences, see "The Turing Trap: The Promise & Peril of Human-Like Artificial Intelligence" (Brynjolfsson, 2022).

However, a fully data-driven business clearly demands extending the concept beyond the operational decision level. Herein lies the problem. As author, Scott Berkun, wrote a decade ago, "Data is not conscious: it is merely a list of inert, dead numbers. Data doesn't have a brain and therefore can't drive or lead anything. At best you want ... (living) decision makers ... [who can] answer good questions about what they're doing, how well it's being done, and what perhaps they should be doing in the future." (Berkun, 2013). This requirement becomes more pressing the higher you go up the decision-making and action-taking pyramid.

At the tactical level, we see the need for more extensive context around data and information. At the strategic level, the requirement for extensive information rather than data adds more significant issues. In addition, at both these levels, being unconditionally *driven* by data leaves little or no room for human judgment, social ethics, or basic flexibility in decision making. **Information enlightened** decisions and human-mediated actions based on contextually rich information and knowledge intuitively offer better outcomes.

This concept of *data driven*—with all its strengths and weaknesses—has today become deeply embedded in the culture and practice of delivering the business' decision-making support needs. And it is from this mindset that the application of AI and ML to decision making and action taking has emerged. Recall that *they* operate solely and exclusively on data; they are truly data driven! Information, knowledge, and meaning are all beyond their ken.

The Action Inputs Model

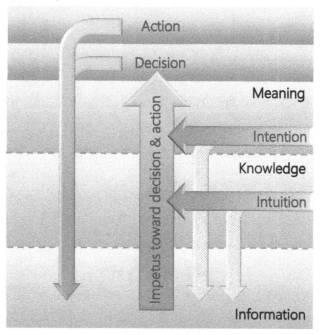

Figure 3.7: The Action Inputs Model

Truly understanding decision making and action taking requires recognition of a set of feedback loops that notionally underpin the entire process. This is described in the Action Inputs Model (AIM) shown in *Figure 3.7.*

We have already discussed the importance of the direct influence of intuition and intention on the impetus toward decision and action. This occurs every time a human engages in the decision-making / action-taking process.

When such decisions and actions occur in a closed-loop digital business, the explicit data outcomes are (or should be) recorded in the information locus for future examination and use, as shown at the left of the above figure. This information may be expected to subsequently feed into AI/ML algorithms and influence their behavior.

However, the same cannot be said of the two feedback paths on the righthand side. In human decision making, recognition of the role of intuition and intention is rare, and its recording even rarer. It may, however, be caught in retrospectives and other formal reviews of decision making, especially where problematic decisions have been taken. In AI-driven decision making, particularly when fully automated, there is no mechanism by which this vital feedback can be captured and used to influence future decisions.

Note further that intention and intuition cannot be fully excluded in AI decision making. Their effects are embedded invisibly in the human-sourced training data of the algorithms. And as (hallucinating) generative AI populates an ever-growing proportion of the internet corpus of training data, the implications could be potentially catastrophic.

Impacts of AI on decision making and action taking

Looking to the current and emerging market for AI in decision making and action taking, as shown in *Figure 3.8* and *Figure 3.9*, the situation gives significant cause for concern.

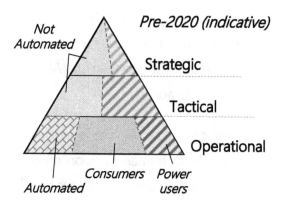

Figure 3.8: Decision making pre-AI

Here, the triangles show the same levels of decisioning and actioning—operational, tactical, and strategic—as seen in *Figure 3.6*. Each level is divided between information consumers (managers and businesspeople) and power users (businesspeople with significant data and/or BI skills), the latter shown by the blue diagonal stripe. A diagonal redbrick pattern is applied where decision making / action taking are being automated; where not, a blue stippled pattern represents traditional data consumer behavior.

The proportions are only indicative, but show that, pre-2020 (*Figure 3.8*), automation is confined to a relatively small percentage of operational decision making. Power users make varying contributions at the different levels. Moving to the present and future (*Figure 3.9*) and based on the forecasts of vendors and AI consultants, the situation changes dramatically. We see AI significantly expanding the amount of automation (the horizontal, redbrick area) of decision making and action taking, displacing consumers' prior work.

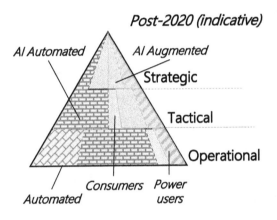

Figure 3.9: Decision making with AI

On the righthand side, the green, solid area represents decision making and action taking that AI is augmenting, for both consumers and power users. The now narrow, blue-stippled area up the center of the triangle shows consumers who continue to do it for themselves. However, the majority of work by consumers and power users is now being supported by AI, improving productivity and increasing insights. This green area is considered a "good" use of AI by most observers.

Here, AI may help with deeper analysis of the supporting data/information, suggest other data of relevance, and make recommendations on how to proceed. People continue to be involved in and ultimately responsible for the decisions made and actions taken.

The horizontal, redbrick area to the left and center is of major concern for a number of reasons. First, AI automation takes control largely or completely out of human hands, significantly reducing or eliminating human oversight of unanticipated social or ethical implications of decisions and actions. Consider, for example, a hiring process—tactical decision making—where AI is used to pre-vet applications. Bias in the AI (as is widely observed) may fully and silently eliminate people of certain races or genders in initial vetting. Hiring managers will be completely unaware of the problem and the applicants will have no knowledge of *why* they have been rejected. Such problems are likely to be prevalent at the tactical level, where much of the decision making undertaken by administrators and middle managers today allows some discretion or judgment. This is of particular concern when the decisions impose financial, social, employment, and similar effects on individual members of the public.

A second concern is that AI automation at this scale eliminates swathes of tasks currently performed by people, reducing businesses' need to employ people to do these tasks.

A typical response to this concern is that these folks can be redeployed to more skilled and higher value work. A more common outcome is, of course, "resource actions". The extent of the redbrick area shown in *Figure 3.9* reflects a belief that bottom-line financial considerations will likely drive AI uptake—as is often the case for new technology. The possible reduction in costs possible through AI-enabled layoffs probably far exceeds any benefits accrued through potentially "better" decisions enabled by AI augmentation.

Cathy O'Neill's excellent *Weapons of Math Destruction* (O'Neill, 2016) predates much the current explosion in AI. However, the examples she gives of the social impact of profit-driven algorithm adoption by business and government remain extremely relevant. They are also extraordinarily revealing of what has already gone wrong as big data and algorithms have been embedded in decision making and action taking processes. It's fair to say that AI and ML are big data and algorithms on steroids.

I'll leave the last words to O'Neill. "Big Data processes codify the past. They do not invent the future. Doing that requires moral imagination, and that's something only humans can provide. We have to explicitly embed better values into our algorithms, creating Big Data models that follow our ethical lead. Sometimes that will mean putting fairness ahead of profit." Just substitute *AI/ML* for *Big Data* and *algorithms* and see the impact increase exponentially.

TAKEAWAYS

- Despite its popularity, there is limited evidence that being data driven easily and directly delivers business value through improved decision making.

- The uptake of BI and related tools has been stuck at 25-35% for decades, suggesting that other factors beyond data and BI/AI tooling play into decision making.

- Rational, evidence-based decision making is far less common than most of us like to think. Rational choice theory, favored by economists and business schools, over-estimates the value of data or information as the basis for many types of decisions.

- Russell Ackoff's DIKW model is too simplistic for modern digital business. Its positioning of data as the precursor of information is particularly problematical.

- The manifest meaning model, m³, proposes three levels (loci) through which we must progress on our way to decision making: (1) the physical locus of data/information, (2) the mental locus of knowledge, and (3) the interpersonal locus of meaning. These become increasingly subjective as we climb the levels. These higher loci encompass real human considerations that contribute to decision making, such as energy levels, emotions, personal and group motivation, and social interactions.

- Data management should really be called (at least) information management, where its true focus lies. It must also consider the higher order concepts of knowledge and meaning as part of its remit.

- Both "single version of the truth" and "single source of truth" are misleading concepts, but for different reasons.

- Crossing the gap from decision to action is a vital *human-centric* and *organization-driven* process that is endangered by a focus on data-driven behavior and today's enchantment with AI.

- Decisions/actions fall into three classes: operational, tactical, and strategic. While decisions at an operational level may well be data driven and amenable to significant levels of automation, those at the tactical and strategic levels demand a much greater degree of context and are better thought of as information enlightened.

- AI operates along a spectrum from automation to augmentation of decision making and action taking.

Automation aligns naturally with operational decisions. Augmentation aligns better with the strategic and tactical levels, where human involvement should be mandatory to account for social and ethical considerations.

- A seldom-considered set of feedback loops within decision making, action taking, intention, intuition, and information will become increasingly important as AI becomes pervasive in decision-making support.

- A significant danger of AI implementation is the urge to maximize return on investment, which is most easily and obviously achieved through automation and a consequent reduction in staff costs. This tends to drive automation up into the tactical and strategic levels of decision making, where it is likely to be problematical for social and ethical reasons, and where human insight and judgment are most clearly and urgently needed.

Chapter 4

DIVING INTO THE DATA LAKEHOUSE

Those that fail to learn from history, are doomed to repeat it.

Winston Churchill

The inventors of the data lakehouse were determined to learn from history. Despite the pitfalls of data warehouse and lake implementations over the previous decade, they could also see that each approach had its strengths. So, in early 2020, Ben Lorica and a group of cofounders and senior engineers from Databricks proposed a data lakehouse[16]. Although other definitions exist, we use their original work as the basis for much of the discussion here.

They described it as "a new paradigm that combines the best elements of data lakes and data warehouses. Lakehouses are

---

[16] The term data lakehouse was apparently first used as early as 2017 by Dr. Jeremy Engle of Jellyvision Lab to describe implementing a combination of lake and warehouse function in Snowflake (Engle, 2017).

enabled by a new system design: implementing similar data structures and data management features to those in a data warehouse, directly on the kind of low-cost storage used for data lakes. They are what you would get if you had to redesign data warehouses in the modern world, now that cheap and highly reliable storage (in the form of object stores) are available" (Lorica et al, 2020).

In brief, warehouse offers the architectural thought, data management features, and appropriate storage structures, while the data lake brings newer underlying technologies. The relative values of these two contributors will become clear throughout this chapter. This is reminiscent of the pattern described in "*Lake + warehouse pseudo-ADP*" and data lakehouse is indeed an enhancement of that approach.

DATA LAKEHOUSE AS DEFINED BY ITS INVENTORS

In addition to the February 2020 blogpost quoted above, Databricks published a further post in August 2021 (Armbrust et al, 2021) that further clarified their thinking on the topic. These two documents together form the basis for our initial swim around the data lakehouse. Note, however, that other vendors, consultants, and implementers have extended and modified these definitions to suit their needs. Some of these approaches will also be discussed here.

A useful glossary definition[17] is also provided by Databricks: "A new, open data management architecture that combines the flexibility, cost-efficiency, and scale of data lakes with the data management and ACID transactions of data warehouses, enabling business intelligence (BI) and machine learning (ML) on all data." The reference to *ACID transactions* may raise a few traditionalist eyebrows, but this will be explained soon. The lakehouse builds on the trends of the 2010s, where data warehouses were being dunked in data lakes with gleeful abandon and limited thought.

Lorica and his coauthors listed eight key features of data lakehouses. They clarify and extend the above definition, forming a sound basis on which to evaluate the pattern.

EIGHT KEY FEATURES OF THE DATA LAKEHOUSE

1. *ACID transactions for concurrent data read and write, to enable and support continuous update.*

   The ACID[18] transactions mentioned above are clarified here. Although ACID has limited application in daily—almost exclusively read-only—use of a warehouse by

---

[17] www.databricks.com/glossary/data-lakehouse

[18] Atomicity, consistency, isolation, and durability (ACID) are properties of database transactions that guarantee data validity despite errors, power failures, etc. en.wikipedia.org/w/index.php?title=ACID&oldid=1173977969

businesspeople, it does apply to the update process. It is particularly important as data ingestion moves from batch to incremental change via streaming, leading to read and write operations by different actors that can and do occur in the same time period.

Identification of this as the first key lakehouse feature confirms a focus on the near real-time operational analytics of events—use cases associated with digital transformation (and "big data")—rather than the still relevant BI and reporting supported by traditional data warehouses fed from traditional operational systems. In fact, both use cases must continue to be supported.

2. *Enforcement, evolution, governance, and auditing for star, snowflake, and other schemata; and reasoning about data integrity.*

This second feature links forcefully to the data warehouse heritage of this new pattern. It drives a need for upfront schema design and levels of instantiation and assimilation completely absent from classic data lake thinking (seen in *Figure 2.6*). The specific reference to star and snowflake schemata, however, may perhaps hint at a limited understanding of the true complexity of the layered, hub-and-spoke data warehouse design that supports subject-oriented, integrated data models.

The mention of governance and auditability is welcome; it also reflects DWC thinking. However, it is limited in the actual design, and the phrase *data integrity* used here cannot be conflated with cross-source integrity (reconciliation), which is a key aspect of traditional data warehouses. Here it means **temporal integrity** within a stream of applied updates coming from the same source.

3. *Use BI tools directly on source data, reducing staleness and latency, and eliminating copies of data, thus lowering the cost of having to operationalize two copies of the data in both a data lake and a warehouse.*

Reducing staleness and latency is a laudable aim, although it applies only to data that is directly streamed into the lakehouse. As we shall see later, more detailed descriptions of lakehouse implementations show a distinctly layered structure. Although these layers could, in principle, be instantiated via database views, in many cases, they appear to be cleansed or otherwise improved "copies" of the base data via batch processes.

Note also that micro-batch loading has been implemented by many data warehouses for more than two decades to reduce latency and staleness. Furthermore, the existence of a single storage technology provides no guarantee that data copies will not proliferate. Indeed, it was the technical debt of multiple, unknown, and un-documented copies of datasets that turned Hadoop data lakes into data swamps. Object storage, as proposed as the foundation of the lakehouse, poses the same challenges as programmers spray data copies all around in their rush to deliver on business goals.

4. *End-to-end streaming to serve real-time reports and data applications.*

The authors assert that real-time reports are the norm in many enterprises. Although true, it must also be noted that time-period reporting, such as daily, weekly, etc., remains necessary and common and often requires consolidation/reconciliation of data from multiple sources.

In the case of these latter reports, end-to-end streaming often does not apply. Streaming into the lakehouse is generally limited to the ingestion data layer, with batch reconciliation processes creating the further data layers needed for such reports or applications.

5. *Open and standardized storage formats, built on object stores, with standard APIs supporting a variety of tools and engines.*

As opposed to data lake storage in raw, as-ingested data structures, open storage formats such as Apache

Iceberg built on object stores offer efficient row-based and columnar storage of data (often with compression), technical metadata storage, and increasingly support schema evolution.

6. *Support all data types ranging from structured to "unstructured" data, including images, video, audio, semistructured data, and text.*

    While the first five points derive from the data warehouse lineage, the last three come from the data lake. The support mentioned here offers nothing beyond the traditional DLC pattern, with all its governance issues.

    It should, however, be noted that all major relational databases, including DB2, Teradata, and Oracle, have long supported a wide range of such data types.

7. *Support diverse workloads, including data science, AI, SQL, and analytics, perhaps requiring multiple tools but all using the same data repository.*

    This may be a key benefit of lakehouse from a business viewpoint. However, how it might be achieved is less clear. It may conflict with some aspects of point 5 (use of open and standardized storage formats, including columnar) because many AI and analytical tool require specific data formats in contrast to the column-oriented structure that is most useful for set-based queries.

Furthermore, all major RDBMSs also support a similar range of workloads and use cases "using the same data repository". This rather contradicts Databricks' claim that this feature is a key differentiator for the lakehouse.

8. *Storage decoupled from compute, for scaling to more concurrent users and larger data sizes.*

This is a typical cloud property[19] but is also seen in or used by some modern relational databases. Given the cloud-native nature of data lakehouse, this would be expected.

Lorica et al offer an evolution story (*Figure 4.1*) for data lakehouse beginning with the 1980s data warehouse and its embedding in a data lake, leading to a multitude of systems and copies of data for different reporting and analytical needs. The figure offers some insight into potential issues with the design. The "Data Warehouse", as drawn, shows multiple warehouses but omits any notion of reconciliation of data from their disparate sources. This carries through to the

---

[19] Data lakehouse could arguably be built on premises, but cloud is the overwhelmingly popular target environment.

"Data Lake" picture. This is actually a data lake plus warehouse pattern but without the different types and levels of complexity seen when ingesting data from traditional operational and cloud sources. This becomes clear when comparing these pictures to the DWC ADP (*Figure 2.4*) and the warehouse and lake pseudo-ADP (*Figure 2.7*).

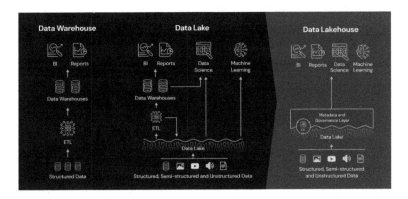

Figure 4.1: Data Lakehouse evolution (Lorica et al, 2020[20])

These leftmost two figures may reflect the big data / external sourcing / cloud / open-source heritage of Databricks' architects. The target "Data Lakehouse" image is a relatively simplistic, high-level picture with obvious shortcomings in how the architecture could handle data coming from traditional on-premises operational environments. A single output from the "Metadata and Governance Layer" sitting atop the data lake is shown feeding BI, reports, data science, and machine

[20] Used with permission of Databricks.

learning. This masks the complexity of the semantic and temporal reconciliation of data required for BI and reporting, as well as the well-known structural differences between these targets and data science and ML. More recent and detailed architectural diagrams of real lakehouse implementations illustrate this complexity in both ingestion (instantiation) and processing (assimilation) into three zones or layers, often labeled bronze, silver, and gold. A set of good (if overly product-focused) examples can be found in "A Cloud Data Lakehouse Success Story" (L'Esteve, 2022).

It is, of course, imperative for many businesses that such legacy data sources be included in the data lakehouse and is therefore shown in the data lakehouse architectural design pattern, even though it adds significant complexity to the design. And it is to this data lakehouse ADP that we must move.

GENERIC FOUNDATIONAL CLOUD ADP

But first, let us redraw the generic foundational on-premises ADP (*Figure 2.3*) for the cloud. *Figure 4.2* shows the cloud version. As one might expect, the only difference between this figure and *Figure 2.3* is the move from separated information pillars to the joined pillars depicting common object storage and the multi-plane representation of cloud and on-premises instances.

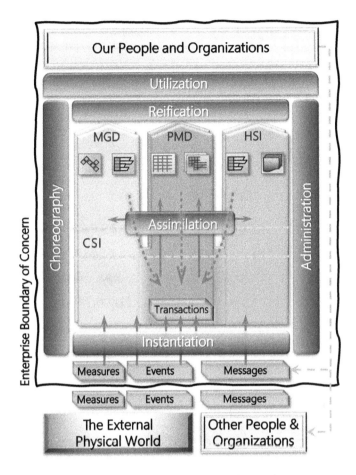

Figure 4.2: Generic foundational cloud ADP

The existence of both cloud and on-premises planes is a key aspect of this foundational ADP. Cloud data warehousing is far too often framed as an exclusively cloud-based implementation. In the real world, the move from on-premises to cloud is slow and, in many cases, never complete. The existence of hybrid cloud/on-premises implementations cannot be ignored, as will be seen later in the emergent ADPs.

DATA LAKEHOUSE ADP

Based on the original Databricks' description and subsequent implementation approaches for data lakehouse, we can now extend and clarify the definition of the data lakehouse ADP given in Volume I, chapter 6.

Data lakehouse ADP definition

Deliver well-integrated BI, reporting, analytical, and machine-learning needs, supporting all data types, as a centralized solution in cloud-native technology. Data storage is based on object stores, supplemented by open-source table formats[21] for structured and semi-structured data, and layered as needed for cleansing, reconciliation, and ease of use. This data is ingested through a streaming function with ACID compliance, managed and accessed equally through SQL-based and analytical / ML tooling, and governed through improved technical metadata support. In addition, support for more loosely structured (so-called "unstructured") data is included, as found in the DLC pattern.

A high-level picture of the data lakehouse ADP is shown in *Figure 4.3*, with added detail in *Figure 4.4* and *Figure 4.5*.

---

[21] See "*Lakehouse information and data storage*" for details of table format stores.

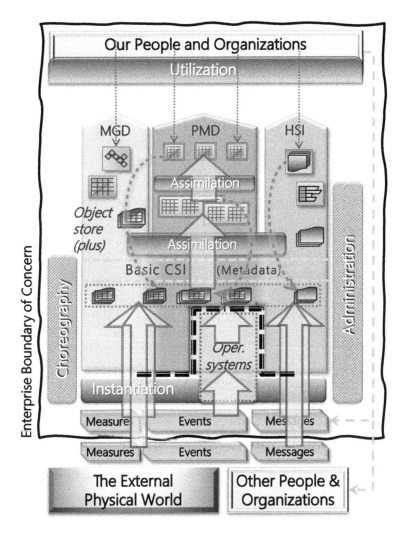

Figure 4.3: ADP: Data lakehouse

Comparing these figures with the lake + warehouse pseudo-ADP (*Figure 2.7*) confirms the lineage of the lakehouse as an evolution of a lake and warehouse combination. Its strength, as argued by its founders, is in its use of cloud-native technology to provide a common data storage and pro-cessing platform for both warehouse and lake needs. Here, the underpinning object storage technology provides the means of uniting the PMD, MGD, and HSI pillars and allowing the formerly separated warehouse and lake stores, seen in *Figure 2.7*, to become a common foundation.

Note my introduction of operational systems as data sources for the lakehouse in the ADP. Few descriptions of the lake-house formally recognize this need, but it is vital when we consider that on-premises operational systems are likely sources of data in more mature businesses.

Figure 4.3 introduces new decorations for the key high-level components of the data lakehouse ADP. Red-brown, dou-ble-outlined arrow shapes link the sources and targets of the various instantiation and assimilation functions into and within the lakehouse. The feed into the operational systems from internal measures, events, and messages is blue to in-dicate that it is unchanged from prior ADPs. These high-level feeds are detailed in the following section.

All three cloud-based pillars are now implemented first in object storage in preference (plus other methods if needed), with object stores depicted by new symbols:

"Basic" object stores

Table format object stores

The dotted line surrounding the set of object stores immediately below the Basic CSI band indicates the initial loading space of the data lakehouse. Note the prior data warehouse block has been broken up into its constituent tables/views, illustrating their closer association with other parts of the lakehouse. These previous warehouse tables/views are colored red and double-outlined to indicate the higher level of governance associated with them as compared to the stores in other areas.

INGESTION INTO THE DATA LAKEHOUSE

Data ingestion revolves around the logical architecture functions of instantiation and assimilation. In addition to external cloud feeds, we must consider operational systems sources. *Figure 4.4* zooms in on this complex set of function.

Measures, events, and messages arriving from different sources, whether external (red brown, triple-line, *dashed* arrows) or internal (red-brown, triple-line, *solid* arrows), all land in the same object storage environment. These arrows represent batch loading (often via scripts) or streaming—of which streaming has become the most common approach in recent years—of data into base lakehouse object stores.

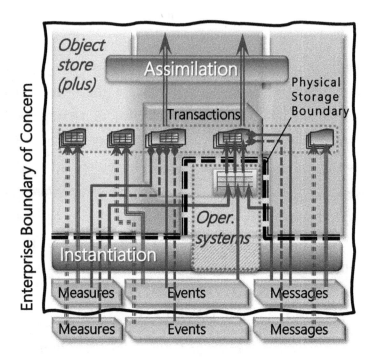

Figure 4.4: Data lakehouse ingestion

For business transactions, the sourcing is varied and extensive. Operational systems, in traditional on-premises environments (the green dotted box), generate and store transactions in relational database systems (the green table icon) as before. These operational systems, separated by a physical storage boundary (the heavy, double-dashed, black line) from the lakehouse, are a key source of transactions in lakehouses fed from traditional on-premises operational systems. Such transactions are ingested into table format object stores within the lakehouse (via the red-brown solid arrows).

In addition, business transactions are generated directly in the lakehouse environment from either internal (via *solid, red-brown, diamond-tipped arrows*) or external (via *dashed, red-brown, diamond-tipped arrows*) measures, events, and messages. These transactions also end up in table format object stores. The surrounding dotted line indicates this area as the landing zone of the lakehouse. (The individual object store icons and the distribution of inputs are illustrative only.)

Of course, generating business transactions in the lakehouse demands the same attention to correctness, consistency, and other quality and governance concerns as applies in traditional operational systems. Such lakehouse-generated transactions also reside in the PMD pillar. Non-transaction data may be stored in basic or table format object stores, the latter facilitating easier integration of data from all sources.

All business transactions, whatever their source, are destined via the red-brown double arrows for the managed and structured warehouse-like tables/views of the lakehouse via assimilation. This function now spreads into both the MGD and HSI pillars to accommodate linking transactional data with other less well-managed data there. This function is often batch in nature because of the need to reconcile data from disparate sources that may arrive asynchronously.

As is evident from the first and fourth of the "*Eight key features of the data lakehouse*" listed earlier, instantiation and, to a lesser extent, assimilation are a focal design consideration of this ADP. This emphasis arises from the data lake legacy of lakehouse. Early data lakes were first filled with externally sourced and relatively unstructured data, often as large files. Manual versioning of these files was possible when data lake usage was limited to batch-based analytics. However, as the nature of big data changed and analytic needs moved toward real time, much of the ingested data became semi-structured, requiring streaming approaches to instantiation. Such processing differs significantly from that of traditional data warehouses, where batches of data from multiple sources are loaded and cleansed, often overnight.

LAKEHOUSE INFORMATION AND DATA STORAGE

The data lakehouse ADP builds on object storage, as does all cloud data warehousing. The driver, as we saw earlier, is to reduce the need for multiple copies of the same data for different use cases.

Native object storage alone is insufficient to handle many of the technical needs for ingesting and managing data with appropriate levels of governance. An additional layer of functionality on top of the object stores is thus required. This is supplied by open-source table formats found in projects such as Apache Iceberg, Apache Hudi, and Delta Lake[22] that offer features such as:

■ *Versioning:* Automatic data change tracking and maintenance of a history of all changes, allowing roll back to previous versions as needed.

■ *Time travel:* The ability to query data as it existed at any prior point in time, allowing tracking of data changes over time.

■ *Data quality:* Built-in data quality checks can detect and fix issues such as null values or data type mismatches.

■ *Support for open-source data formats:* Objects can store significant amounts of technical and structural metadata, allowing open-source, column-oriented data file formats, such as Apache Parquet and Apache ORC (Optimized Row Columnar), to be constructed within them.

■ *ACID support:* When streaming record-level data into the lakehouse, ensuring that data remains consistent and accurate over time is vital. ACID (Atomicity, Consistency, Isolation, Durability) support is the basis for this. Note

---

[22] Databricks also offers a proprietary, more functional fork of Delta Lake.

that ACID support is only on a per-table basis and does not (yet) support multi-table transactions.[23]

These features are enabled by the inclusion of significant levels of technical metadata within the underlying file structures. Iceberg, Hudi, and Delta Lake are evolving and offer differing features, using different technical approaches for metadata support. Details are beyond the scope of this book, but Dremio's Alex Merced provides a deeper dive (Merced, 2022) with ongoing updates up to August 2023 as of this writing. These extended table format object stores are particularly valuable in storing business transactions, as well as MGD.

A recent technology and market analysis of data lakehouse by dbInsight (Baer, 2023) offers further understanding. The conclusion is that open-source table formats, built on object stores, are the direction for data lakehouses and that the market is likely to narrow to two contenders in the future, with Apache Hudi the possible loser as many major data warehouse vendors plump for either Iceberg or Delta Lake.

---

[23] ACID is a common error prevention and recovery feature of databases. Experience shows that delivering fully functional, reliable ACID may take many years because of the hundreds of unique error conditions that may never occur in testing.

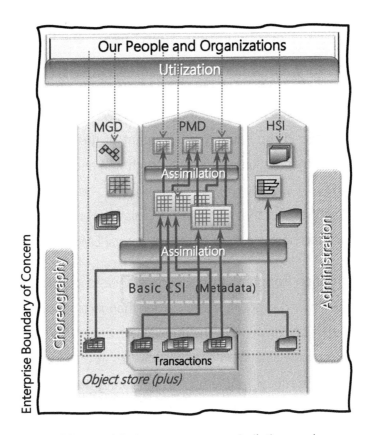

Figure 4.5: Data lakehouse storage, assimilation, and access

Turning to *Figure 4.5*, we note a layered structure in the PMD pillar reminiscent of traditional data warehousing. These layers are identified (Heintz & Lee, 2019) as ingestion tables (bronze), refined tables (silver), and feature/aggregated data stores (gold). In "6 Guiding Principles to Build an Effective Data Lakehouse" (Walter et al, 2022), they are named as raw, curated, and final. The curated layer is defined as holding cleansed, refined, filtered, and aggregated data, while the final layer reflects business or project needs. The final layer in this description aligns closely with the concept of data marts. However, the curated layer, as defined by Walter et al, differs from an EDW in that it contains aggregated data. This divergence in the naming and content of the upper layers indicates that thinking about the structuring and governance of data in a lakehouse is still evolving. As experience grows, we might expect that layering in the data lakehouse will approach the best practices of the traditional DWC pattern.

Assimilation from bronze to silver and then to gold is generally batch and programmatic (rather than streaming) in nature. This is a result of the inevitable time-dependent aspects of reconciling data from different sources. It thus introduces similar or identical problems with delivering the most timely data to businesspeople, as has long been identified with the data warehouse classic ADP.

Figure 4.5 also shows that files and datasets continue to exist in a standalone manner, as seen in the data lake. The improved function and expanded scope available from the technical structure of table formats (where appropriate), and from modern metadata tools do allow for improved governance. However, descriptions of the data lakehouse place very limited emphasis on how these traditional data lake components can be integrated with or linked to the core warehouse.

They simply exist in the same object store and are thus more easily available to access or use.

Basic CSI (metadata) is now shown as beginning to extend into all three pillars in accordance with the logical architecture. A plethora of open-source tooling, such as Apache Atlas, Amundsen, DataHub, and Linux Foundation Egeria is emerging. However, although expanded to some extent in the lakehouse over prior warehousing implementations (especially compared to the data lake), much of the focus remains on technical metadata, and currently does not extend to the full scope of context-setting information (CSI) envisaged in the architecture. When the three pillars coexist in a single, cloud-based environment, this expansion of metadata scope is easier in some respects, and it may be expected to continue further. However, including hybrid on-premises and multi-cloud implementations leads to a highly distributed CSI environment, complicating management and sharing.

The choreography and administration components of the logical architecture are not focus areas of data lakehouse design at present, and they remain limited in scope and features. Similarly, reification is not addressed in the data lakehouse ADP, meaning that data is accessed in individual and separate sets from utilization. Some descriptions of data lakehouse do include a virtualization function. In our patterns approach, we show that as one of the key features of the data fabric ADP.

Returning to *Figure 4.3*, three data reverse flows are shown. Two are from the higher layers in the PMD pillar to the ingestion layer, as was discussed in "*Data Warehouse Classic/op ADP.*" The third reverse flow in the HSI pillar represents the model management common in analytics and ML applications. (It also exists, but is not shown, in the MGD pillar.) Such reverse flows are vital to the improved operationalization of analytics and are, of course, simplified by the location of all data in the same environment. However, reverse flows from the lakehouse back to on-premises operational systems remains as difficult as ever. Such reverse flows are seldom discussed in any detail in data lakehouse implementations in the literature. They have differing challenges and will need careful consideration in detailed design.

EVOLVING THE DATA LAKEHOUSE CONCEPT

As previously noted, the data lakehouse concept was first formulated by Databricks, a software vendor with a decade of history in the world of "big data." Its founders were part of the AMPLab project at the University of California, Berkeley, from which Apache Spark emerged, and Databricks remains a major contributor to this project to this day. Delta Lake, (unsurprisingly) built on Spark, is Databricks' flagship data lakehouse implementation. As a result, a Databricks lakehouse implementation does *not* include a formal relational database management system (RDBMS) at its core.

Since 2017, Databricks has maintained a close relationship with Microsoft, who has also become a strong supporter of the data lakehouse concept. In addition to supporting Databricks' Delta Lake approach, Microsoft also offers the option to have an RDBMS, Azure Synapse Analytics, at its heart (see Korkrid, 2020, for example).

James Serra, a long-time data warehouse expert, has labeled these differing approaches as *NoEDW* and *ProEDW,* respectively (Serra, 2021). He comments: "... if you are trying to make a data lake work like a relational database, why not just use a relational database (RDBMS)?" With cloud RDBMSs based on table format object stores and the lakehouse concept spreading to all cloud platforms, the use of a true RDBMS at its core seems likely to become widespread.

Martyn Jones, who has been involved in data warehousing since its inception, took a contrarian and deeply dismissive view of data lakehouse soon after it appeared. His rant begins: "Move over big data hubris and data lake stupidity there's a newer, thicker and far bigger a***hole on the block. And it goes by the unbelievably idiotic name of data lakehouse" (Jones, 2020). Beneath the polemic, Jones contends that data lakehouse is a purely technological solution built on the "big data" software ecosystem that previously failed to deliver a real business-driven, high-quality data management environment supporting decision making. His argument is certainly valid in reference to the starting point of the concept. However, as it has evolved, some more data management intelligence has fleshed out the technological skeleton. Nonetheless, the data lakehouse concept continues to overly rely on technological solutions rather than considering the broader data management picture.

Strongly supporting the data lakehouse from a data management perspective is no other than Bill Inmon, who has published three books on the topic. Inmon's approach to the data lakehouse is in a straightforward, easy reading style that will be very familiar to his many readers, beginning from his earlier work on data warehousing and on through textual and unstructured warehouses and data lakes. Both *The Data Lakehouse Architecture* (Inmon & Srivastava, 2022) and *Rise of the Data Lakehouse* (Inmon & Srivastava, 2023) start with an explanation of three types of data—structured, textual, and analog/IoT—that are included in the data lakehouse. The authors describe their conceptual attributes: structured data is aligned to traditional high-level data warehouse concepts; textual is defined in terms of Inmon's previous work on textual disambiguation; and analog/IoT is basic event streams. These types partly reflect the PMD, HSI, and MGD pillars we use here.

At this point, however, the authors diverge fast and far from the data lakehouse concept described by all its other proponents, as well as from the ADP discussed here. Inmon and Srivastava contend that "there is absolutely no reason why we need to house all the data in the data lakehouse on the same technology. Some data can be on the cloud, some on premise. The physical housing of the data is not a problem as long as the analytical infrastructure is built and maintained properly." The analytical infrastructure turns out to be, in essence, all the context-setting information (CSI), including a canonical model, that describes and relates all the data in the lakehouse wherever it resides. When any analysis is required, it may be necessary, they say, to extract and combine the data needed into a "single physical pool" of data. This description sounds more like data fabric than data lakehouse.

A recent global study of C-suite executives, chief architects, and data scientists by MIT Technology Review (MIT, 2023) reports that "Nearly three-quarters of surveyed organizations have adopted a lakehouse architecture, and almost all of the rest expect to do so in the next three years... Ninety-nine percent of lakehouse adopters say the architecture is helping them achieve their data and AI goals."[24]

However, these remarkably high figures should be contrasted with the analysis presented in Gartner's "Hype Cycle for Data Management" (Rosenbaum, 2023), which puts lakehouse market penetration at 5% to 20% and describes it as "adolescent" in terms of its maturity. A possible explanation may be that the MIT study executives were perhaps conflating the use of S3 object stores with data lakehouse adoption.

DATA LAKEHOUSE ADP—CONCLUSIONS

Based on the analysis here and the opinions of the experts above, we summarize the strengths and weaknesses of the data lakehouse ADP and come to some high-level conclusions about its value and applicability to real-life situations. Note, however, that the ADP is based largely on the original specifications by Databricks. Many implementers and vendors have adapted and expanded from that starting point, so it will be necessary to consider these pros and cons in the light of your specific situation.

---

[24] *Full disclosure:* report produced in partnership with Databricks.

Pros of the data lakehouse ADP

- This ADP is technically underpinned by a separation of storage from processing and a full adoption of parallelism, elasticity, and other cloud approaches.

  Data lakehouse is optimized to use cloud storage and cloud-native processing technology, fully supporting the move of informational systems from proprietary, on-premises environments. This aligns with the reality that increasing quantities of data originate in the cloud and that technology advances now occur first in the cloud.

- Data lakehouse is built on low-cost, scalable, but lower performing object storage for all data types.

  The use of a single storage technology in data lakehouse may reduce data redundancy in comparison with separate or combined data lake and warehouse implementations. BI/reporting and analytical/AI share the same base data, reducing data management costs and increasing interoperability between these different approaches. However, stringent data management will be required to achieve the goal of reduced data redundancy.

- By incorporating open-source table formats at a file and record level, data lakehouse adds many (but not all) database management techniques typically absent in object storage.

Open-source table formats, such as Apache Iceberg, Apache Hudi, and Delta Lake enable ACID compliance when ingesting data via streaming technologies. They also provide a strong basis for immutable, historical data (where updates do not overwrite existing values) and schema evolution as business needs change and evolve.

- **Data lakehouse supports the relational storage models on which BI/reporting is based and the raw detailed data structures demanded by analytics and AI.**

Column-oriented storage structures, such as Parquet and ORC, enabling fast set-oriented queries are supported in the lakehouse, in addition to more record-oriented structures used in analytics and AI, mirroring the evolution of data structuring seen in traditional data warehouses over recent years.

- **ACID transaction support is highlighted in this ADP, enabling improved information preparation in some aspects of the lakehouse.**

With streaming as a primary ingestion method in the lakehouse, the ACID compliance enabled by table formats, such as Apache Iceberg, etc., is vital in ensuring the temporal integrity of event processing. It is also important for the ELT (extract, load, and transform) processing applied when moving data between bronze, silver, and gold layers/zones. However, it should be noted that ACID delivered by these non-database mechanisms may take some years to fully mature.

- **Data lakehouse addresses some of the more worrying "data swamp" issues seen in traditional data lakes.**

The focus on structured and semi-structured data in the lakehouse provide opportunities for improved data governance and management in comparison to what is possible in traditional data lakes. This would require the adoption of data catalogs and other metadata function, focus on which is limited to more technical aspects in the data lakehouse definition.

CONS OF THE DATA LAKEHOUSE ADP

- **Data lakehouse design has emerged from a starting point of externally sourced, semi-structured "big data".**

Data lakehouse ingestion emphasizes event streaming from individual data sources and, therefore, does not often address typical data warehouse ingestion from multiple sources (including operational systems) where reconciliation of data across these sources is mandatory.

The skills required are those typical of web / open source / Hadoop developers with less focus on the types of data management skills seen in traditional data warehouses. These latter skills are, of course, vital in any data warehousing solution.

- **Consideration of migration from an existing, traditional data warehouse (DWC/op) to a lakehouse is limited.**

  Following on from the starting point described in the previous bullet, there is limited experience among data lakehouse proponents of migrating from traditional, on-premises data warehouses—with all their sourcing and data integration complexity—to a lakehouse. The most common approaches seem to assume that data from operational system sources is "just the same" as externally sourced data, an assumption that is likely to fail dramatically in many cases.

- **Some data lakehouse implementations lack a comprehensive RDBMS.**

  Some data lakehouse implementations favor the use of a full-function RDBMS at the heart of the lakehouse. Others, principally Databricks, prefer to build such function in a unified multi-language engine, such as Apache Spark, to achieve maximum engineering flexibility and open sourcing (Olinloye, 2022). However, this latter approach may lead to a lack of the full range of RDBMS function, such as referential integrity, multi-table transaction support, and so on. It also places all data tasks on the programming community, leaving out the business users of BI tools.

- **Data lakehouse proponents seldom focus on data governance and related concerns.**

  The design and evolution of the data lakehouse pattern is heavily technology driven. Implementers typically come from a software engineering background, with specific expertise in open-source and cloud-based systems, often operational or siloed analytical in nature. Often absent is a strong grounding in data management or even databases. As a result, data governance considerations may be under-emphasized.

- **There may be a reliance on immature or emerging software to build some aspects of the data lakehouse, especially in cases where no relational database is used.**

  A consequence of the software engineering background of many data lakehouse proponents is their willingness to live with both the strengths and weaknesses of open-source software. The result may well be systems management issues as open-source projects are born, grow, and die over time. Basing such a complex and interconnected environment as a data lakehouse on such shifting foundations is risky.

DATA LAKEHOUSE ADP: IS IT YOUR DESTINATION?

The data lakehouse ADP offers the basis of a valid and viable cloud data warehousing solution in support of the business drivers of providing a foundation for decision making and action taking. To answer the question posed in the title above, we must focus on the features described in the "*Data Lakehouse ADP*" section and the accompanying pictures. And we must ignore vendor marketing, grandiose success stories from the internet, conflating aspects of fabric or mesh with the lakehouse, and experts bending the concept to their own agendas. So, what is your journey and how could you best undertake it?

The starting gate

Enterprises with existing data lake and warehouse combinations (see "*Lake + warehouse pseudo-ADP*") are best positioned to undertake this journey. You are likely to have a good mix of data lake technology skills and experience in the data management needs of data warehousing. If your solution is already in the cloud, even better.

Other starting points include enterprises with either a data warehouse on premises or in the cloud (DWC/op or DWC/cn ADPs), or an existing cloud-based data lake (DLC ADP).

The journey

The underlying business need addressed by the data lakehouse ADP is to integrate traditional BI and reporting needs with those of analytics and machine learning. When the analytics are heavily operational, the lakehouse is asked to span both operational and informational environments. And if your enterprise has evolved from a traditional bricks-and-mortar world, this integration will likely cross the divide between on-premises operational systems and a growing cloud environment.

All this leads to the highly complex ingestion approach shown in *Figure 4.4*. It is necessary to tackle the technological challenges this presents at an early stage and in depth. However, it may be easy to get too focused here. Much of the literature emphasizes these aspects. Of (arguably) greater importance are data management issues, from modeling to metadata, as well as a well-considered data governance strategy.

If you arrive from a "true" data warehousing approach (see "*Data Warehouse Classic ADP*"), this will come naturally. If your background is more from data lake or cloud implementation in general, the technology may come easier, but data management will be key to longer term success.

The destination

The data lakehouse ADP offers a well-bounded and implementable solution to the broad church of cloud data warehousing needs—insofar as any data warehouse can be called *well-bounded!* Combined with a technological foundation that is becoming increasingly mainstream, this relatively manageable and self-contained implementation is one of the strengths of its centralized approach. Of course, centralization also has its weaknesses. Attempting to address these weaknesses is a key driver in both the other patterns: data fabric and data mesh. It is to data fabric that we next turn.

TAKEAWAYS

- A data lakehouse is described by its inventors as "a new paradigm that combines the best elements of data lakes and data warehouses... implementing similar data structures and data management features to those in a data warehouse, directly on the kind of low-cost storage used for data lakes... cheap and highly reliable storage (in the form of object stores)".

- Eight key features were identified by its founders. Analysis of these features provides a first understanding of the fundamental characteristics of a lakehouse. Two key aspects are the inclusion of ACID characteristics for data ingestion and the use of open-source table formats built on object stores as a common basis for both warehouse- and lake-like data storage.

- In an evolution of the initial thinking, a layered data structure—often labeled bronze, silver, and gold—has emerged to handle cleansing, integration, and specialization of data. It is similar, but not identical, to the layering seen in the traditional DWC pattern.

- The data lakehouse ADP is defined as delivering well-integrated BI, reporting, analytical, and machine-learning needs, supporting all data types, as a centralized solution built on cloud-native technology. This data is ingested through a streaming function with ACID compliance, as well as batch support for on-premises operational sources. It is managed and accessed equally through SQL-based and analytical/AI tooling and governed through improved technical metadata support. Support for more loosely structured (so-called "unstructured") data is also included, as per the DLC pattern.

- Many current implementations focus on ingestion of streaming events from the external cloud environment, demanding ACID compliance to ensure the temporal integrity of the incoming data. The full data lakehouse ADP deliberately extends this focus to include traditional on-premises operational systems as first-class sources. This should always be considered as a starting point for design, although it adds processing complexity to support batch-based delivery of such data and the need to reconcile it semantically and temporally across sources. However, these traditional sources are likely to persist for many years to support long-standing business processing in many traditional industries.

- There exist many alternative descriptions of data lakehouse from vendors and experts that diverge from the principles outlined by its founders and the general consensus on architecture and function that is represented by the data lakehouse ADP defined here. While this consensus may evolve, it now appears fundamentally stable.

- The main strengths of this ADP stem from its use of well-defined cloud-native technologies for data processing and enhanced object storage as a common foundation. This offers a solid existing base for implementation and scope for technological evolution.

- The main weaknesses of this ADP also stem from the same technological base that emerged from operational and siloed analytical, cloud-based systems. This leads to a relatively poor understanding and application of data management principles and data governance approaches. It is also reflected in the limited focus on metadata beyond the technical level. With its extensive technology dependencies, lakehouse implementers should consider the future danger of unacknowledged, and perhaps unrecognized, technical debt.

- The lack of a true RDBMS in many designs to deliver fundamental relational function may lead to excessive bespoke and costly development by many implementers. Avoiding the use of an RDBMS seems a sure recipe for technical debt.

- The most likely starting point for your journey to a data lakehouse is from an existing data lake + warehouse pseudo-ADP, from which the lakehouse ADP is a clear evolution.

Chapter 5

Unraveling the Data Fabric

*A generation which ignores history
has no past – and no future.*

Robert A. Heinlein

The proponents of data fabric were likely as determined to learn the lessons of history as their data lakehouse counterparts. The pitfalls they were keen to avoid were different and their starting point distinct from those of the lakehouse and, as a result, the solution differs in significant ways. Nonetheless, data fabric and data lakehouse can be viewed as complementary patterns. In fact, some marketing materials conflate the two in ways that may confuse potential implementers. However, some simple architectural positioning is all that's required to resolve any misunderstanding.

Data fabric, as a term, dates further back than data lakehouse. Early references can be found as far back as 2016 at least, when the phrase was used by Forrester (as Big Data Fabric), and in a manner that clearly presages its more recent emergence: "Big data fabric offers enterprise architecture (EA) pros a platform that helps them discover, prepare, curate, orchestrate, and integrate data across sources by leveraging big data technologies in an automated manner." (Yuhanna, 2016). It was also adopted early by various software vendors, where it was often linked to data virtualization.

With the demise of "big data" as marketing's most-favored message, data fabric became Enterprise Data Fabric (Yuhanna, 2020) or, more simply, data fabric (Ghosh, 2019) toward the end of the last decade. Ghosh provides a good definition of data fabric as "a distributed data management platform, where the sole objective is to combine various types of data storage, access, preparation, analytics, and security tools in a fully compliant manner, so that data management tasks become easy and smooth." Beyond stating the key driver of data fabric, this definition also implies the challenges it addresses: Data management is neither easy nor smooth when the business need is for integrated real-time analytics and BI/reporting.

Unlike data lakehouse (and data mesh, as we shall see), no one specific date or paper marks the "birth" of data fabric. However, the event that propelled data fabric into the top three of cloud data warehousing approaches was probably its listing as one of Gartner's "Top 10 Data and Analytics Trends for 2021" (Panetta, 2021). It is to Gartner's definition of data fabric that we next turn for an initial and relatively comprehensive, modern exposition.

DATA FABRIC AS DEFINED BY GARTNER AND OTHERS

In "Data Fabric Architecture is Key to Modernizing Data Management and Integration," Gartner labels data fabric first as a "design concept that serves as an integrated layer (fabric) of data and connecting processes" (Beyer, 2021). The phrase *design concept* may cause some concern to systems implementers. Two definitions may clarify. WIXEncyclopedia offers[25] from a web design point of view that "a design concept refers to the idea or plan that guides the design decisions being made in a specific project." Airfocus, with a product management focus, suggests[26] "a design concept is the core idea driving the design of a product, explained via a collection of sketches, images, and a written statement." We may conclude that Gartner is aiming to provide no more than an overall envelope within which designers and developers of software and systems will contribute components to data

---

[25] www.wix.com/encyclopedia/definition/design-concept/

[26] airfocus.com/glossary/what-is-a-design-concept/

fabric. However, describing it "as an integrated system of data and connecting processes" takes us no further than a high-level, conceptual/logical picture that could describe any type of cloud data warehousing. Or indeed any data provisioning system for any purpose.

So, what are the key design principles that constitute the data fabric concept as per Gartner? A data fabric:

- *Uses continuous analytics of metadata*—discoverable, existing, or inferenced.

    Placing this initial emphasis on ongoing analytics of metadata—or, more correctly, context-setting information (CSI)—sets the foundation for data fabric. Ongoing and universal discovery and use of CSI will enable all the following aims.

- *Supports integrated and reusable data*—across all hybrid and multi-cloud environments.

    Data in this concept exists in all environments and it must be both integrated and reusable for maximum value.

- *Enables* **access to data in place** *or supports its* **consolidation** *where appropriate*—supporting the creation and use of data across multiple environments.

The aim is not to consolidate all data on to one platform, nor is it to insist that all data must be accessed and used where it is found. Data fabric recognizes that both techniques are needed and must be supported in a modern digital business.

- *Identifies and connects data from disparate sources*— creating an integrated data/information resource.

  Recognizing that business depends on information from multiple sources, many of them not designed to work together, and some poorly defined, data fabric aligns to the type of integrated, reconciled, and modeled resource identified in the IDEAL conceptual information thinking space[27].

- *Discovers unique, business-relevant relationships*—contextualizing data into information for added value.

  Taking the previous point to a business level, data fabric supports converting data into information through AI/analytics pattern discovery techniques and recording the resulting CSI and information for business use.

---

[27] See Volume I, chapter 3 for details of the conceptual architecture.

- *Leverages human and machine capabilities*—blending human experience with AI pattern discovery.

  There is no suggestion that AI can solve all the problems of data management, although its strengths in pattern discovery will be vital in automating data management. People must still be fully involved.

- *Supports re-engineering of decision making*—providing more value than traditional approaches through rapid access and comprehension.

  The business outcome of data fabric is improved decision making based on universal access to better managed and contextualized data from disparate, heterogeneous sources.

There's much to like and aim for in the above principles. But how can they be achieved?

KEY PILLARS OF DATA FABRIC

Beyer, in the above article, offers a graphical view of five key pillars[28] from data sources to consumers of a "comprehensive data fabric." Taken from the graphic, they are [*my italics*]:

---

[28] Called *pillars*, they look like layers to me. Did the pillars fall over? ☺

1. Data catalog—to access and represent all metadata types in a *connected knowledge graph.*

2. Analytics over the connected knowledge graph—to "activate metadata."

3. AI/ML algorithms enriched with *"active metadata"*—to simplify and automate data integration design.

4. *Dynamic data integration*—to deliver integrated data through multiple data delivery styles.

5. *Automated data orchestration.*

The highlighted terms do not have generally accepted meanings across the industry and, unfortunately, are not defined in any detail by Beyer. As a result, a variety of definitions and descriptions of what data fabric means have emerged from analysts, consultants, and software vendors. Forrester, for example, says that data fabric "focuses on automating the process integration, transformation, preparation, curation, security, governance, and orchestration to enable analytics and insights quickly for business success" (Yuhanna, 2020). DZone proposes that "data fabric architecture is a distributed data management approach that enables organizations to integrate, manage, and analyze data from various sources, including on-premises, cloud, and edge environments, in a seamless and unified manner. It provides a flexible and scalable framework that allows organizations to adapt to changing data requirements and rapidly capitalize on new business opportunities" (Patnaik, 2023). IBM suggests "data fabric is an architecture that facilitates the end-to-end integration of various data pipelines and cloud environments through the use of intelligent and automated systems" (IBM, 2023).

We may note that the consultants' definitions are often vague. Vendors' definitions, on the other hand, focus on the breadth and strengths of their product sets. IBM's product set is extensive and their definition accordingly broad. Vendors of more focused products define data fabric more narrowly to suit their offering. So, how do you decide if a data fabric might meet your needs?

My approach here is to attempt to consolidate the various more common definitions into an architecturally meaningful and consistent superset. The seven principles above, together with the five (albeit loosely defined) key pillars, provide the foundation for a conceptual image of data fabric that aligns well with the emerging industry consensus. This conceptual image will then form the basis for defining a data fabric architectural design pattern.

DATA FABRIC—A CONCEPTUAL IMAGE

At the core of data fabric is metadata, or as I prefer to call it, context-setting information (CSI). It sits at the heart of *Figure 5.1,* repeating the design explored in Volume I, Figure 4.3.

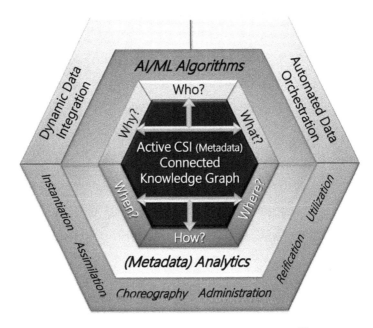

Figure 5.1: Data fabric—conceptual view[29]

Data fabric specifies, in addition, a technological foundation for CSI storage and management: a connected knowledge graph. Knowledge graphs are an important emerging

---

[29] Note: the color scheme of the CSI hexagon and interrogatives has been updated to blue to emphasize that CSI is *information,* while the surrounding hexagons show *process.*

technology[30], and data fabric envisages this technology as its base. No rationale for prefixing *knowledge graph* with *connected* is offered, but it may be intended to suggest that both the business information and CSI are instantiated and linked in a single graph.

But what does *active* mean in this context? According to Lewis Wynn-Jones of ThinkData Works (a data catalog platform vendor), "**active metadata** implies that both the metadata itself and [its] management are active... First, metadata should change as the data itself changes. As data is used, updated, and modified, metadata should be continuously generated, collected, and indexed. Second, the traditional management of metadata should be automated through APIs, enabling a rapid, collaborative approach to metadata management." These two points are at the core of what active metadata really means.

The contrast to traditional, "passive" metadata is clear. Active metadata / CSI is intimately connected to business data/information and its changes in real time through agile, automated processes. It is distributed across all the systems where the data/information resides. Therefore, it enables all aspects of managing such data/information in real time too.

---

[30] See Volume I, chapter 5 for further details.

Surrounding this core in *Figure 5.1* is a shell of (metadata) analytics and AI/ML algorithms. In data fabric, analytics over base, passive metadata helps to build the graph connections and continuously monitors ongoing change in the environment to activate the metadata. As we shall see in the next section, active CSI (metadata) in a connected knowledge graph is the first technological foundation of data fabric. This forms the training data for AI and ML algorithms that provide advanced predictions of emerging data management and integration needs.

The two functions in the outer shell—dynamic data integration and automated data orchestration—operate based on this active metadata. These functions clearly relate to the process components of the logical REAL architecture shown in *Figure 2.2*. We explore the details in "*Comparing terminology.*" For now, we simply list the REAL process functions—instantiation, assimilation, choreography, administration, reification, and utilization—in the lower section of *Figure 5.1*.

The mindful reader may recall that the technology underpinning some of the REAL process functions—choreography, in particular—could be described as emergent. Data fabric is accordingly challenged. Nonetheless, its starting points can be seen, to varying degrees of evolution, in three broad classes of technology and products, as we shall see in the following section.

Note also that data fabric does not specify any specific data storage or processing platform. In fact, it is clearly platform agnostic and asserts that the data/information required to support decision making and action taking resides in multiple, disparate stores across a hybrid, multi-cloud environment; and must be integrated to serve these needs. This immediately echoes the drivers of one of our foundational ADPs: logical data warehouse. These thoughts underpin the ADP definition offered later in "*Data fabric ADP.*"

DATA FABRIC—TECHNOLOGICAL FOUNDATIONS

Beyer's five key pillars align only partially with the technologies that are used by vendors offering data fabric solutions. In real implementations, we see three foundation technologies. These are: (i) connected knowledge graphs, (ii) information preparation, and (iii) information access. We discuss these topics in turn.

As a design concept promoted by large analyst firms, such as Gartner and Forrester, data fabric has been adopted by many vendors as a foundation for product marketing. These vendors broadly fall into one of these three foundation categories. In addition, some larger vendors offer products that span two or all of the categories. Vendors and products mentioned here are no more than examples, current as of this writing. This should not be construed as promoting any vendor mentioned or dismissing any omitted.

CONNECTED KNOWLEDGE GRAPH

Gartner's description of converting all kinds of passive metadata—technical, business, operational, and social—to active metadata (Beyer, 2021) focuses on the creation of a connected knowledge graph from data catalogs[31] and/or business glossaries, the former more IT oriented and the latter more business focused. There exists a plethora of both long-standing and recently emerged solutions, including Alation, Apache Atlas, Collibra, Dataedo, erwin, Octopai, and Zeenea, as well as offerings from all the big data management vendors. However, metadata integration across tools and platforms has long been a challenge. Recent open-source approaches to this include the DataHub platform, the Egeria project[32], and the inclusion of self-describing tables in Apache Iceberg.

Before turning to knowledge graphs, we should explore why context-setting information (CSI) is such a better term than metadata in understanding the concept of *activation*.

---

[31] Sometimes called *metadata catalogs*.

[32] datahubproject.io/ and egeria-project.org/

CSI identifies the purpose of "metadata" (in its broadest sense) as setting the context for data/information use and explicitly defines it as information rather than data. *Figure 5.1* shows the range of interrogatives that CSI must address. The top set—why, who, and what—relate mainly to the primary business driver of CSI. The part of Beyer's definition of *activation* as "depict[ing] metadata in an easy-to-understand manner, based on their unique and business-relevant relationships" is thus already inherent in CSI. The bottom set of interrogatives—when, how, and where—apply more to the technical areas of CSI that are fundamental to automating orchestration and driving dynamic integration. The question of *when* leads to consideration of the different levels of temporality of CSI and what that means for activation[33].

Business-level CSI changes at a sedate pace. How often do we change business capability definitions or information ownership? Probably yearly at most. On the other hand, technical-level CSI, particularly in the operational area, is highly dynamic. How often might the quality indicators on ingested data change due to loading or processing errors?

---

[33] Note that this is analogous to the evolution of our understanding of business data. Early systems recorded the business in an "eternal now" (and data modeling has reflected this for decades). Only with the emergence of decision-making support did we need to consider how to manage the changing and historical aspects of data/information.

Potentially daily or even more frequently. Activation of CSI, therefore, must reflect the cadence of changes in the underlying CSI if it is to adequately support both automated orchestration and dynamic integration. Active CSI is thus continuously, if unpredictably, changing CSI.

Similar considerations of business-focused vs. technical CSI apply to the connected knowledge graph. Let's first explore business-focused CSI. A knowledge graph is an abstraction layer that provides a common business understanding of the data/information used by the business, based on ontologies—formal definitions of data objects and their interrelationships—both externally sourced and internally generated. This supports both self-service data access and analytics.

Andreas Blumauer's presentation "Introduction to Knowledge Graphs and Semantic AI" gives an excellent overview of this topic and is the source for *Figure 5.2*.

While clearly more tourist-driven than business-centric, it shows the sort of information and relationships that would clearly meet Beyer's requirement for an easy-to-understand view of unique and relevant business information and its interrelationships. People and places are linked through multiple relationships, such as visits, likes, ratings, and so on. Various characteristics of places—images, coordinates, opening hours, etc.—are recorded in a user-friendly way.

W3C ontologies and languages (top right) ensure a common vocabulary and base set of known information. In the case of a business, this is far more than one might expect from a simple business glossary. This connected knowledge graph represents how the business and its information work; in some limited sense, it is a digital twin of the business.

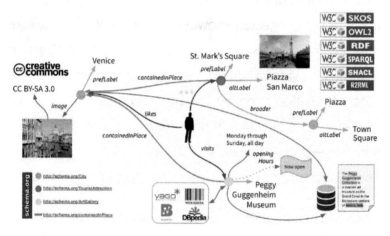

Figure 5.2: Conceptual knowledge graph (Blumauer, 2019)

Technical CSI is also easily represented in a knowledge graph or series of linked knowledge graphs. A traditional data catalog containing data governance metadata, such as data elements contained in datasets, can be mapped to the technical infrastructure (app servers, cloud instances) on which the datasets reside and the apps and services that update them, as well as to the physical locations where they are located. An outage in a particular location and its impact on specific data elements can be traced through the technical

CSI, automated workarounds initiated, and the owners and users of the relevant information alerted.

In traditional data warehousing, technical metadata is mainly passive in nature: it is manually collected and documented and used "off-line" by IT and data governance teams in data catalogs to understand and manage the environment. Similarly, business glossaries are often static representations of the way business uses the data. Such a sedate and hands-off approach is incompatible with digital transformation, and data fabric seeks to address this by automating all aspects of CSI collection, analysis, change management, etc.

At the business level, this includes changes in the use of data by the business, both planned and organically evolving; revisions of rules or changes in legal constraints; and organizational changes, from job changes and departmental realignments to mergers and acquisitions. Where possible, this should be driven directly from the business systems that implement these changes rather than through manual processes that are often delayed or sometimes forgotten. In effect, this combines the semantic layer from many BI tools, databases, and catalogs into the knowledge graph. However, the effort in adjusting the consolidated information, correcting the underlying repositories, etc. should not be underestimated.

Every change in the IT systems that affects data/information must be tracked automatically (as far as possible) in the technical CSI. This includes updates to information preparation processes, changes in physical data locations, hardware and software upgrades—all of IT service management. Ongoing, automatic capture of operational metadata—completed tasks and error situations, performance issues, and more—is also mandatory. Operational analytics, supported by emerging AI function, is envisaged as spanning the entire, distributed CSI environment, learning from existing metadata, and predicting what data management actions are needed to keep the business data/information fresh and correct.

All this active CSI is grist to the mill of knowledge graphs. We described the concepts and techniques in Volume I, chapter 5 as part of our discussion of emerging approaches to information storage and context setting. With data fabric, these techniques have been applied in products such as Cambridge Semantics' Anzo and Stardog's Enterprise Knowledge Graph platforms[34]. The activated and connected CSI/metadata in platforms such as these drive the next two foundational technologies: information preparation and information access. But first... some terminology.

---

[34] cambridgesemantics.com/anzo-platform/ & stardog.com/platform/

COMPARING TERMINOLOGY

Data warehousing products have traditionally been split into those that *prepare* the data/information for use and those that provide *access* to it. This is illustrated in *Figure 5.3*. The REAL logical architecture retains the distinction, and provides underpinning functional components used by both. Information preparation is performed in the instantiation and assimilation functions, supported by choreography and administration. Information access consists of utilization and reification, also aided by choreography and administration. Active CSI is recorded by, drives, and links all these functions.

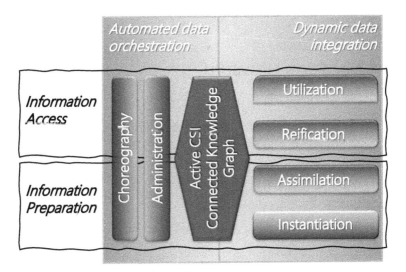

Figure 5.3: Data fabric—comparing terminology

As the industry has focused increasingly on (near) real-time decisions, this horizontal split has become less obvious. Data fabric builds on this new thinking and the key pillars of dynamic data integration and automated data orchestration do not distinguish between preparation and access. However, the technologies required and the products that deliver them are generally more easily described and understood in terms of information preparation and information access and the REAL functional components shown in *Figure 5.3*.

Furthermore, as implied in the following two sections, many vendors of data fabric solutions define data fabric exclusively in terms of either information preparation or information access, based on the capabilities of their existing or planned product sets.

INFORMATION PREPARATION

The operation of the instantiation and assimilation functions[35] has been explored extensively in the discussion of the foundational and data lakehouse ADPs in Chapters 3 and 4. Data fabric neither affects nor changes these methods or operations in any significant way, bar one. Rather than traditional manual management, data fabric proposes that these functions must be dynamically managed and automatically initiated and operated based on the active metadata in the

---

[35] For further detail of the underlying methods see Volume I, chapter 4.

connected knowledge graph. Nevertheless, human review is a necessity in the early stages of adoption.

There is currently no agreement between data fabric proponents nor even a common description of how that might be done. Every vendor offering data fabric solutions promotes specific approaches aligned with their product offerings. In a market lacking a sufficiently defined or agreed design of this aspect of data fabric, we must fall back on the theory that informed the REAL logical architecture. There, providing dynamic management and automated initiation of tasks (or services) is the function of choreography, supported by administration.

Choreography is defined as providing the framework for microservices or service-oriented architecture (SOA) methods to enable workflows to be constructed on the fly from independently defined and built tasks/services (well bounded functional units). While choreography, in a general sense, coordinates and orchestrates the actions of *all* participating tasks/services of the REAL architecture to produce the desired business and/or technical outcomes, the focus for data fabric is on information preparation and access.

Adaptive workflow management

Choreography supports the creation, management, execution, and monitoring of a system of workflows or processes consisting of independent, disparate services and activities. Workflow management has traditionally focused on well-understood, predefined workflows of optimized and computerized tasks, common in highly structured production environments—insurance claims handling, for example. Digital transformation, on the other hand, demands far more variability and innovation, and thus more sophisticated, flexible workflows combining highly variable tasks, both computerized and manual. This leads to the concept of **adaptive workflow management** shown in *Figure 5.4*.

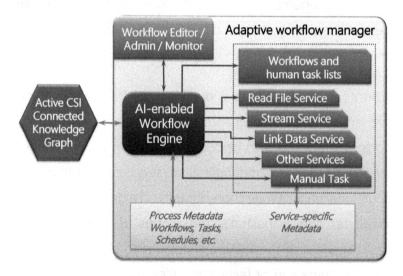

Figure 5.4: Adaptive workflow management

At the core of adaptive workflow management—optimized here for information preparation—is a workflow engine, which provides execution-time support for all aspects of the workflow, including initiating services in the active workflow, exception handling, performance monitoring, and so on. It also generates and manages human task lists.

Workflow models, definitions, and rules are created in the workflow editor and stored as process metadata/CSI. The workflow engine provides administration and monitoring functions. Definitions of services and their interfaces are also part of the CSI stored in the workflow manager. This CSI-based, rule-driven approach allows IT to define and modify workflows via administration. More importantly, for the automation required by data fabric, it enables their definitions, structures, and components to be analyzed and changed via AI algorithms, providing a highly adaptive environment.

The above image is conceptual and speculative. Such function is still emergent in the market, with multiple vendors defining and delivering it differently and offering greater or lesser portions of the required solutions for data fabric. Solutions in this space include Talend's Data Fabric, Tibco's Cloud Integration, and Apache Airflow[36].

---

[36] www.talend.com/products/data-fabric/, airflow.apache.org/, and www.tibco.com/products/cloud-integration

INFORMATION ACCESS

Of data fabric's three technological foundations, the conceptual and product underpinnings of information access are by far the most mature. Dating to the earliest days of data warehousing—under a variety of names and scopes—information access came into prominence in the early 2000s under the name **data virtualization**. It's also known as enterprise information integration (EII) or data federation. In the REAL logical architecture, the functionality is called reification, supported by CSI and assimilation.

Reification provides consistent, cross-pillar, real-time access to data/information according to an overarching model. It serves two purposes:

1. It offers various real-time access methods to retrieve data/information from disparate data stores, converting it to a common form, usually SQL.

2. Where data/information must be joined from various stores, it provides a mediating layer with semantic interpretation and matching, schema translation, and so on.

Together, these two functions support real-time joins between data in stores with differing levels of temporality and/or structure. For example, customer service agents may require a combination of verified and reconciled historical contact and account data in the data warehouse, up-to-the-minute account status from operational systems, and the messages exchanged with the customers in a content management system. Reification allows this without the need to create yet another store of derivative data consolidated in advance. However, reconciling these data sets in real time depends on the existence of a current set of semantic and temporal models of the underlying sources and their contents. Architecturally, this is CSI and assimilation is the function that creates and manages it.

In product terms, data virtualization tools (in their more advanced forms) provide all the function described above. A typical architectural representation is shown in *Figure 5.5.* Reading from top to bottom, queries in a variety of forms (of which only a subset is shown) from businesspeople and their various applications and tools are fed into the query engine. There, individual queries are split into sub-queries based on knowledge of where the data is stored and how it must be optimized to perform in the networked environment.

This knowledge comes from the metadata (CSI) stored in the data virtualization environment. The resulting sub-queries are distributed to source data stores of a wide variety of formats. Reading upward, returned results may be cached for future performance enhancement. They are recombined in the federation engine before being returned to the requesting app or businessperson. *Figure 5.5* also shows the active CSI/metadata connected knowledge graph of data fabric as a key source/target of metadata within the tool.

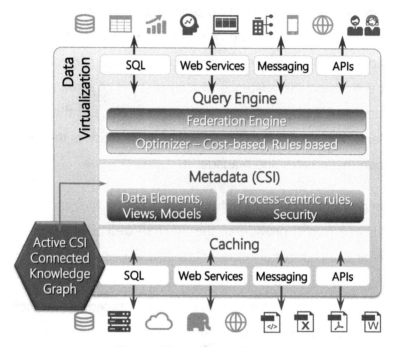

Figure 5.5: Data virtualization

Data virtualization has been regarded with some suspicion by many proponents of data warehousing. Much of this is based on specific and real concerns:

▪ Can *your* data be integrated on the fly?

As is well known from traditional data warehousing, the preparation, cleansing, and reconciliation of incoming data to create semantic and temporal consistency can be complex[37]. These same challenges apply to data virtual-ization with two added twists. First, the integration must be done in near real-time. Second, the outputs must be consistent with any integration performed when loading or updating the warehouse by batch, replication, or streaming processes. These concerns have long caused data warehouse proponents to reject data virtualization, despite its clear benefits when access to data beyond the warehouse—especially real-time data—is required.

- **Security and privacy concerns**

Security and privacy issues, including compliance with verifiable semantics, also arise. The data warehouse has long provided an ideal platform to apply security and manage such issues. Direct access to operational systems is risky, especially in financial institutions or where OLTP (on-line transaction processing) is provided via legacy systems on mainframe platforms.

- **Performance characteristics**

Performance aspects of users' queries traversing net-works with variable response times prompt questions:

---

[37] See instantiation and assimilation in Volume I, chapter 4 for details.

o Is there sufficient network bandwidth dependably available to support the variable and potentially large data sizes being transported from remote locations?

o Can the network offer predictable response times and, if not, is that acceptable to businesspeople?

o How efficient and dependable is query optimization for mixed / distributed data volumes? To provide effective optimization, the metadata describing the network and its current state, as well as data models and volumes must be accurate and up to date.

o Other worries about specific data virtualization tools may include how effectively they use massively parallel processing and caching.

o Finally, and perhaps most importantly, data warehousing professionals know that legacy source systems are often very sensitive to queries for which they were not designed and so ask about possible impacts on response time for operational transactions.

- **Data sources**

Although data virtualization tools offer many connectors to a wide range of source system, there may be one vital source you need that is not supported. Similarly, there may be new sources, such as Apache Iceberg, that have only recently emerged.

Solutions for information access include Denodo and TIBCO Data Virtualization, as well as componentry embedded in many major data management vendor platforms. Newer, highly scalable tools like Starburst also include virtualization and add distributed optimization[38].

DATA FABRIC ADP

The above analysis of the technologies at the heart of data fabric enables us to define the most appropriate architecture design pattern. What is perhaps most obvious is that data fabric has little or nothing to say about the data/information that it serves to the business. There is no mention of data storage technologies, such as we saw in the data lakehouse ADP. Nor do we find definitions of different types of structures for different purposes, such as the EDW and data marts of the DWC pattern. Data fabric simply accepts that a multitude of data stores of diverse natures on many platforms is required by the modern business.

---

[38] www.denodo.com/en/denodo-platform/denodo-platform-80/
www.tibco.com/products/data-virtualization/
www.starburst.io/.

The data fabric ADP, shown in *Figure 5.6*, is thus defined as offering enhanced management and automation of information preparation and access, supported via full-function REAL process components. This is supported via extended, AI-enhanced active metadata/CSI that reflects the actual, changing, live business and computing environment across all pillars of data/information and all processes.

This definition differs from that offered in Volume I, which stated that the data fabric ADP was usually centered on a DWC. Although many data fabric implementations do indeed have a data warehouse or lakehouse at their core, it is more correct to say that the pure data fabric ADP is agnostic to the data/information stores and their underpinning structures. This is indicated in *Figure 5.6* by graying out the entire information space—its pillars and data stores—except for context-setting information, which is highlighted as the connected knowledge graph.

Although it remains true that the data fabric ADP is an evolution of the logical data warehouse (LDW) ADP, the lack of a mandatory data warehouse at its core marks data fabric out as a new species. The focus has shifted fully from information to process. This shift of emphasis reflects the fact that it was in the arrows of data flow between subsystems where the largest costs are historically found. This occurs because the data flows often include substantial data transformations to satisfy a new point of view, a new semantic, or the formation of more complete analytics contexts.

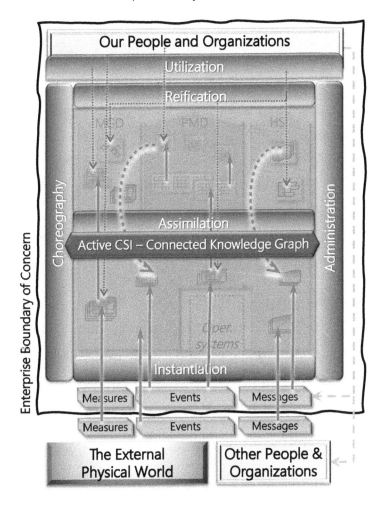

Figure 5.6: ADP: Data fabric

The foundational DWC and LDW ADPs depend on instantiating a data model to reconcile data from multiple sources. However, this construct is resistant to change, leading to significant challenges in a fast-moving digital business. The data fabric ADP pushes this model into context-setting information and activates it via analytics and AI. At least in theory, this adds the flexibility and agility required.

As a result, it is the *process components*—utilization, reification, assimilation, instantiation, choreography, and administration—of the REAL logical architecture that become key to this ADP and are highlighted and now fully conjoined in *Figure 5.6.* The three types of function they support—information preparation (solid blue arrows), information access (dotted blue arrows), and reverse flows (curved dashed arrows)—are equally emphasized.

Of course, data fabric is still an emerging pattern, and it should not be assumed that tools and products delivering the above process components necessarily include all the functionality required by the full logical architecture. However, the data fabric ADP provides significant steps toward the full intent of the processes envisaged there.

DATA FABRIC ADP—CONCLUSIONS

Having explored the evolution of data fabric from analyst exposition to functional analysis, let's now summarize the strengths and weaknesses of the data fabric ADP and come to some high-level conclusions about its value and applicability to real-life situations.

Pros of the data fabric ADP

- Data fabric offers a comprehensive and focused approach to preparing and accessing data from all the diverse sources required by a modern digital business.

The foundational data warehouse ADPs focus first on the data stores and structures required for business decision making and action taking; information preparation and access processes then derive from this. Data fabric starts from a generic approach to the creation and management of these processes, irrespective of the specific data stores or structures desired. The result is a powerful and generally applicable set of function that can be applied to a warehouse or lakehouse, and all the disparate sources of data that the business needs.

- Data fabric shows a clear evolution from existing systems.

With its origins in industry analyst firms, data fabric is based on a good understanding of what a broad range of current products offer and their development plans. We, therefore, see a clear evolutionary path from existing systems to the more extensive function of data fabric.

- **The result is an extensive set of supporting vendors.**

  Vendors from areas including traditional data preparation, ETL and ELT, data virtualization, data catalog, and
  knowledge graphs, as well as the big data management
  vendors, have all enthusiastically embraced data fabric as
  a go-to-market approach. This leads to a broad range of
  mainstream tools and products that support this ADP
  and ongoing work to embrace its future vision.

- **Required skills are generally available.**

  With broad market support and multiple products, development and maintenance skills are widely available.

- **Well-defined methods and organizational approaches
  for information preparation and access are used.**

  Existing, well-understood methods and organizational
  approaches are directly applicable to the implementation
  of information access and preparation in data fabric.
  However, implementers will need to get to grips with
  new skills and methods in the area of activating metadata
  and populating and using connected knowledge graphs.

- **Knowledge graphs and active metadata are the distin-
  guishing technologies needed to achieve a data fabric.**

These technologies unify the fabric and orchestration of data flowing between the multiplicity of systems found in modern data warehousing environments.

Cons of the data fabric ADP

- **Some specific key aspects of the software stack for data fabric are still immature and/or emerging.**

  Metadata has long been the Achilles' Heel of data management for data warehouses and data lakes. Data fabric (correctly) places it front and center in automation and adaptive management of information preparation and access. However, despite advances in AI/ML and increasing interest in knowledge graphs and semantic ontologies, these are still at an early stage of adoption. In addition, orchestration/choreography of workflows remains immature.

- **Data catalogs and metadata standards continue to lag in required function and interoperability.**

  In addition to the previous point, we note that the metadata standards required for interoperability between different catalogs have proved difficult to agree on and gain acceptance across vendors. In highly disparate multi-cloud and hybrid environments, this may prove increasingly challenging.

- **Data fabric's seeming lack of novelty may make it difficult to sell in the face of current data management challenges.**

  The similarity (at least on the surface) of data fabric to logical data warehousing and its support by many traditional data warehousing vendors may cause forward-looking organizations to dismiss it as "tried that once, didn't like it!" That would be unfortunate, as it has much to offer in moving data management to an adaptive and automated approach.

DATA FABRIC ADP: IS IT YOUR DESTINATION?

The data fabric ADP does not, on its own, fully support the business drivers of providing a foundation for decision making and action taking. Rather, it addresses the growing problem of providing an adaptive and automated process environment for information preparation and access. And it offers to tame the numerous problems of distributed databases, lakes, and files.

To answer the question posed in the title above, we must focus on the features described in the "*Data fabric ADP*" section and the accompanying picture, but recognize that it will need to be underpinned by a data warehouse classic (DWC/cn) or lakehouse ADP to address the design and implementation of the data/information platform. So, what is your journey and how could you best undertake it?

The starting gate

Given the conceptual resemblance of data fabric to the logical data warehouse, it should be immediately clear how to start your journey to the data fabric ADP if you already have the experience of and skills in delivering a logical data warehouse. However, as mentioned, the data fabric ADP does not mandate that you adopt a particular approach to data storage and structuring, so you may decide to stick with your existing data warehouse core (on premises, for example) or move to a DWC/cn or data lakehouse ADP at the same time, depending on your appetite for risk. The key business need is, as ever, to provide a core of reconciled, historical data for decision making and action taking.

If you are starting from a centralized DWC/op (without logical data warehouse functionality) and moving to the cloud with either a DWC/cn or data lakehouse approach, you will very likely need to carefully consider your needs for distributed information preparation and access, especially if your target (or interim) destination includes both cloud and on-premises function. In this case, the data fabric ADP should be included in your planning.

The journey

The fundamental drivers of the data fabric ADP are to max-imize the agility and automation of the plethora of infor-mation preparation and access processes that underpin a modern, highly distributed digital business. Cloud data ware-housing is a primary beneficiary of this drive, but other as-pects of your digital transformation efforts will also profit.

In the case of cloud data warehousing, the choice of sup-porting ADP—DWC/cn or lakehouse—may drive further de-cisions on technology choices within data fabric. Data lakehouse implementations lean more toward the open-source technology stack than the more traditionally imple-mented DWC/cn. The latter is more likely to be supported by more integrated data fabric solutions from larger vendors. A blend of traditional database tools will have to coexist with myriad separate solutions provided by cloud vendors.

The largest challenges in data fabric implementation in all cases are likely to center around metadata/CSI—its collec-tion, its integration across platforms, and its activation via AI/ML processes. The extent to which your chosen knowledge graph provider can support these activities will be an important consideration.

The destination

The data fabric ADP, supported by your choice of DWC/cn or data lakehouse, offers a comprehensive solution to cloud data warehousing needs. Its starting point from existing products (and their vendors' plans) and its base in well-understood—although still emergent—technology should give a high level of confidence in this ADP as implementable in the medium to long term and a relatively future-proof solution to your cloud data warehousing needs. And be prepared to evolve the fabric in your organization at a rapid pace.

TAKEAWAYS

- Early references to data fabric date to 2016, at least: the phrase *Big Data Fabric* was used by Forrester in a manner that is clearly aligned with its more recent use.

- Ghosh defines data fabric as "a distributed data management platform, where the sole objective is to combine various types of data storage, access, preparation, analytics, and security tools in a fully compliant manner so that data management tasks become easy and smooth." (The latter goal may be optimistic ☺ .)

- As adopted by Gartner and other analysts and vendors, data fabric is a design concept that begins by applying analytics and AI to basic metadata to activate it. This becomes the basis for automating the integration of data across hybrid and multi-cloud environments and enabling access to data in place with maximum agility.

- Five key pillars are identified: (i) a data catalog and connected knowledge graph of metadata, (ii) analytics to activate this metadata, (iii) AI/ML algorithms to simplify and automate data integration design, (iv) dynamic data integration across multiple data delivery styles, and (v) automated data orchestration.

- A conceptual view of data fabric equates active metadata in a connected knowledge graph with the context-setting information (CSI) component of the REAL logical architecture, making it central to dynamic data integration and automated data orchestration.

- Implementing a data fabric is most easily understood in terms of three technological foundations: (i) connected knowledge graph, (ii) information preparation, and (iii) information access—also known as data virtualization. There exist software products of varying degrees of maturity supporting all three technological foundations.

- The data fabric ADP offers enhanced management and automation of information preparation and access, supporting data/information management in a diverse, distributed environment, supported via extended and AI-enhanced active metadata that reflects the real, changing, live business and computing environment across the entire set of data stores and processes.

- The data fabric ADP's strengths are its powerful approach to preparing and accessing data from all required, diverse data sources and its evolution from existing vendor products that enables existing skills and development methods to be applied.

- Its weaknesses stem from the relative immaturity of some of its metadata-related underpinnings, a steep learning curve for standard ontologies by business, and a dependence on metadata interoperability standards that have long struggled to gain general acceptance.

- An existing logical data warehouse offers the most likely starting point for implementation of the data fabric ADP. However, to fully support cloud data warehousing business needs, it must be paired with either a DWC/cn or data lakehouse ADP to provide the central core of reconciled, historical data.

Chapter 6

UNTANGLING THE DATA MESH

I like the dreams of the future
better than the history of the past.

Thomas Jefferson

It may well be that the proponents of data mesh agree with Thomas Jefferson in his above preference. Certainly, of the three emergent architectural design patterns, data mesh is the most dismissive of the history of data warehousing and dreams most deeply of a distributed future. Indeed, in the very first article introducing the term in 2019, Zhamak Dehghani pleads with her readers "to momentarily suspend the deep assumptions and biases that the current paradigm ... has established," (Dehghani, 2019).

Titled "How to Move Beyond a Monolithic *Data Lake* to a Distributed Data Mesh" *[my italics]*, the author asserts that the historical approach to data warehousing is problematic while conflating data warehouse and data lake. This misconception is common among implementers of data lakes of the past decade, as discussed in "*Lake + warehouse pseudo-ADP.*" Beyond causing some long-standing data warehouse experts to throw the article aside, it also hints at issues with the data mesh approach that will be discussed later.

As requested by Dehghani, we try to keep an open mind as we explore her criticisms of the "current enterprise data platform architecture" and her proposals to address the problems. However, many of her claims will be fiercely (and correctly) disputed by those who have experienced or delivered successful data warehouses. The following sections draw deeply on her two seminal posts (Dehghani, 2019 and 2020) and her book, *Data Mesh, Delivering Data-Driven Value at Scale* (Dehghani, 2022).

DATA MESH—PROBLEM AND SOLUTION

THE PROBLEM IS...

Data mesh is proposed as a new enterprise data architecture for today's reality, where data is "*ever present, ubiquitous and distributed.*" This is set in contrast to the existing data platform architecture, which is "*centralized, monolithic and domain agnostic*" (Dehghani, 2019). The evolution of this prior architecture is described in three generations:

- The first generation of enterprise data warehouses, based on proprietary platforms that have left a huge technical debt of thousands of unmaintainable batch ETL jobs understood only by a small, centralized team of highly specialized engineers.

- The second generation of data lakes built on "big data" technologies and populated by long running batch jobs, maintained by centralized, hyper-specialized engineers.

- The third generation, similar in approach to the second, but characterized by streaming real-time data and unified batch and streaming transformation, all in the cloud.

In contrast to the comprehensive history in Volume I, this set of three generations is hugely simplified. It strongly emphasizes the highly centralized nature of data warehouses and lakes, both in their physical structures and the specialized teams that maintain them. A further focus on the technical approaches to information preparation "pipelines" entirely misses the need for cross-source data reconciliation prevalent in the (first generation) DWC ADP that was also largely lost in the DLC pattern of the second and third generations. Nonetheless, the characterization of prior architectures as monolithic and centralized is unarguable, at least prior to 2010. The charge of them being *domain agnostic* centers around the technology-focused nature of the engineering teams (*domain* has a very specific meaning in data mesh, as we shall see in "*Domain ownership of (analytical) data*").

Architectural failure modes

Dehghani identifies three architectural failure modes:

1. ***A centralized and monolithic platform that can support neither proliferation of data sets nor innovation.***

   The data warehouse or lake environment hosts and owns data from all sources and offers it to all targets. Its designers and engineers do not understand or care about the business drivers or information context of either the source or target systems. This lack of knowledge creates a bottleneck to innovation in the business and struggles increasingly as data sources and targets proliferate.

2. ***Coupled pipeline decomposition requires rework of the full pipeline for the smallest changes in business needs.***

   The functionality of information preparation is split into stages according to mechanical functions—such as ingestion, cleansing, aggregation, and serving—delivered by separate teams. However, these stages are highly coupled, such that small business-driven changes ripple through the stages, creating significant maintenance challenges for each stage team in turn.

3. Siloed, hyperspecialized ownership of different parts of the information creation process.

The teams responsible for the source and target systems know and are driven by the different business needs of these systems. The source team often has little incentive to provide quality data beyond its own area. The team responsible for the warehouse/lake platform specializes in data engineering and lacks any real business understanding of the data they receive and provide. The target team seldom has any deep understanding of the original data sources.

The problem identified by data mesh is that centralization—both physical and organizational—as found in all prior data warehousing solutions, is a bottleneck to addressing rapidly changing business needs where data is ubiquitous, rapidly growing in volume and variety, and widely distributed. This presents readers with a classic example of a false dilemma between centralization and distribution. Neither approach is inherently good or bad. Good architecture demands a blend of both, not a choice of one over the other.

It is also worth noting that the problem is initially detailed (Dehghani, 2019) in terms of information preparation and access—ETL and specifically pipelines. This leads to a strong focus on the process and people thinking spaces of the conceptual IDEAL architecture[39], in contrast to the stronger consideration of the information thinking space seen in the earlier DWC patterns and in the data lakehouse ADP.

AND THE SOLUTION IS BASED ON...

In her 2022 book, Dehghani classes data mesh as a "sociotechnical paradigm." Architecturally, it is strong on conceptual principles, of which there are four, introduced briefly in this section. Data mesh is not (yet) a fully-fledged logical architecture. The functions described remain at a relatively high level, and interpreters (like myself) and implementers of data mesh are left to speculate on and assume how some aspects can be realized in practice. As Dehghani states in the prologue: "it's too early in the life of data mesh to describe an example of a company with a mature data mesh, as we are currently in the process of building the first data meshes" (Dehghani, 2022).

The four principles that underpin data mesh are:

1. Domain ownership of (analytical) data

Analytical data ownership is aligned with the "business domain" closest to the data, either its source or its main

---

[39] For details, refer to Volume I, chapter 3, "Three thinking spaces for cloud data warehousing."

consumer. Business domains are based on the thinking of Eric Evans in his seminal *Domain-Driven Design: Tackling Complexity in the Heart of Software* (Evans, 2003).

2. *(Analytical) data as a product*

Data is managed as if it were a physical product, with a product owner responsible for its quality, production, and evolution, with a goal of seamless sharing. The product is a **data quantum** (defined later) that encapsulates all the data, metadata, code, and policies needed to deliver it to its users/customers.

3. *A self-serve data platform*

A platform and set of services designed to empower domains' cross-functional teams to share data without friction from design and creation to consumption.

4. *Federated computational governance*

Data governance operates in a federated manner with minimal central guidance and based on practices that codify and automate the policies at a detailed level and are embedded in data products and platform services.

My added parenthetical *(analytical)* in the first two bullets emphasizes where data mesh focuses versus the broader use and benefits of both concepts in the operational world.

DATA MESH—PRINCIPLES AND PRACTICES

The above four principles form the heart of data mesh thinking but may be unfamiliar to many traditional data warehousing practitioners. We now dive deeper to explain each principle and explore their strengths and weaknesses in early practice, as well as describing contrary opinions.

DOMAIN OWNERSHIP OF (ANALYTICAL) DATA

Domain-driven design (DDD) is an important software design approach (Evans, 2003). It focuses on modeling software to match a **domain** according to input from that domain's experts. In DDD, a domain is a "sphere of knowledge, influence, or activity" (Evans, 2015) corresponding to the business subject area of a piece of software. A domain consists of one or more **bounded contexts,** within each of which a semantic model and a common, ubiquitous language are shared between all participants. Domain-driven design has been highly influential in software systems architecture over the past twenty years and has been widely applied in designing operational (transactional) systems on modern platforms. It has also led to the widespread acceptance of microservices.

Data mesh applies DDD thinking to informational systems, and to analytical systems in particular. This is a response to the belief that the major problem for analytical systems delivery and change resides in the way the pipeline of data from operational sources to informational targets is split between different teams with varying organizational demands and skills. This problem is expressed in the latter two "*Architectural failure modes*" and shown in *Figure 6.1(a)*.

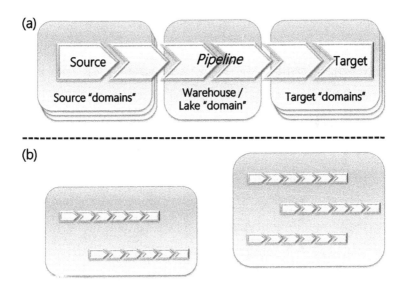

Figure 6.1: Data mesh domain thinking

Here, control and development of a virtual pipeline (in its broadest sense) of data from its operational sources to its informational targets is split into domains longitudinally by technology base: source and extraction on the left; combination[40] and transformation in the middle; and loading and

---

[40] I have deliberately avoided the term *reconciliation* here because data mesh does not address this need explicitly.

analysis on the right. The quoting of *domain* in this figure indicates that these are not domains envisaged by Evans.

Dehghani says of traditional data warehousing approaches: "We have moved away from *domain-oriented data owner-ship* to a *centralized domain-agnostic data ownership.* We pride ourselves on creating the biggest monolith of them all, the big data platform." Historically, domain-oriented data ownership postdates by a considerable time the monolithic EDW; so, "moving away" is misleading. However, centralized domain-agnostic ownership is at the core of lakes and ware-houses and is certainly the current paradigm and source of many challenges. The solution, according to data mesh, therefore, is to adopt true domain-oriented data ownership across the entire analytical data environment and embed in-dividual and separate pipelines within the resulting domains, as shown in *Figure 6.1(b)*.

The key challenge, however, is to define useful domains with associated bounded contexts. Modern operational sys-tems—designed according to DDD—may have well-bounded business contexts, defined by the business out-comes required and constraints placed on their software de-velopment projects. However, many legacy systems span or conflate multiple contexts, as seen in the major ERP plat-forms. Likewise—but for different reasons—informational systems, both analytical and BI/reporting, are typically loosely, if at all, bounded, specifically because their exploratory nature may lead them to who knows where.

Data mesh—arbitrarily, it seems—chooses as its domains what could be called business functions, basically following the seams of organizational units as bounded contexts, on the basis that the language of a business function is common and shared. For clarity, we call these **business domains**. This choice aligns governance and development responsibilities with the business and, thus, with drivers of change.

However, four challenges immediately arise. First, at what level in the organization do we set these boundaries? We could choose to align with the C-level responsibilities and have a small number of very broad business domains, such as finance, sales, logistics, etc. Or we could choose many more, smaller, more focused domains with smaller teams and tighter ubiquitous languages. Second, what will happen to existing domains when the organizational structure changes, as it inevitably will? Data mesh does not offer answers for now.

Third, this exclusive focus on domains based on business functions excludes (or at least, obscures) some common informational needs. Most obvious is the need for cross-functional reporting and analytics. In addition, what about other domain definition criteria that may also be appropriate, such as geographical, legal, or product categorization.

The fourth challenge can be phrased as: How "far back" into the operational environment do these business domains constructed for analytical purposes stretch? Data mesh admits that existing operational systems differ in nature from the datasets needed for analytical work. As we shall see, data mesh also respects this traditional operational/informational split, placing itself firmly in the informational environment. However, when discussing the details of domains' component parts, the domains are shown as including both operational and informational function.

We might conclude that Dehghani paints a "to be" destination that is worthwhile but, in many situations, is impractical.

In this context, Ben Stopford's article, "The Data Dichotomy: Rethinking the Way We Treat Data and Services" (Stopford, 2016) is informative. He frames the data dichotomy as: "Data systems are about exposing data. Services are about hiding it." (Micro)services are the modern approach to designing operational systems and their aim is to hide (encapsulate) their data. Legacy operational systems have a similar—if unstated—aim, although their scope is far broader than that of services. Data warehousing, in contrast, is all about exposing data. This dichotomy begs the question: how suitable is a highly encapsulation-focused mindset for data warehousing? An answer must await our exploration of the structure of data products in the next section.

However, data mesh's clear preference for non-centralized approaches to design has led it to DDD, which is service oriented at its core. A further area of concern is that Evans' concept of Strategic Design rejects the possibility of a completely unified domain (business) model as neither feasible nor cost-effective. Rather, he proposes that a domain consists of multiple, **independent** models, each within a defined bounded context and contextualized within the particular domain. DDD then introduces **context mapping**, which explicitly defines the relationships between these models within their bounded contexts. This means the different user/developer domain teams may share data context, hide context, or conform to one group's definitions. Within data mesh, these bounded contexts (and their models) and context mapping form the basis of data products and the relationships between them, as discussed next.

(ANALYTICAL) DATA AS A PRODUCT

In the data warehousing community, the concept of data as a product has aroused considerable interest and excitement, even beyond proponents of data mesh. Conceptually, the idea of a data product conjures images of successful commercial products, with qualities such as dependability, value, feasibility, usability, etc.—iData, anybody ☺ ? In short, they *delight their customers*, an outcome for which data warehouse and lake developers might be prepared to kill.

In data mesh, these goals are approached in a very specific way. Analytical data products are defined as self-contained, autonomous, and coequal participants in a distributed, federated mesh. Their mandatory characteristics: they should be discoverable, addressable, understandable, trustworthy and truthful, natively accessible, interoperable and composable, secure, and valuable in their own right. Each of these attributes is relatively self-explanatory, but for an in-depth discussion, the reader is referred to Chapter 3 of Dehghani, 2022.

To deliver on these attributes, a data product must be owned and managed by a **product owner** within a business domain. As with any product owner, the goal is to ensure the product's customers' needs are met or exceeded, that the product is of the highest quality, and that there exists an ongoing focus on evolving and improving all aspects of the product over time. For customers of data in today's data warehouses and lakes, such goals likely appear as magical thinking. Hence, the universal welcome for data as a product.

Data as a product changes the relationship of teams to the analytical data they create and use. Data is built to be shared rather than collected and siloed. A culture of data-driven in-novation is facilitated by the easy availability of high-quality analytical data, supported by the existence of explicit con-tracts between teams to ensure that data changes in the source do not impact data consumption. However, today's data engineers' skills and experience are of process and pipelines rather than product related. Data as a product de-mands the latter to be successful.

The preceding discussion centers around the intangible na-ture and organizational effect of treating analytical data as a product. At a functional level, data mesh introduces the **data product quantum** (or data quantum, for short). This is de-fined as encapsulating all the data of the product as well as the code that maintains it. It is also self-describing in terms of semantics and syntax, thus containing all the metadata/ CSI to make it discoverable and usable. And it contains the contracts and interfaces (also known as input and output data ports) for access in all available modes. In this encapsu-lation of data, CSI, code, and interfaces, the data quantum echoes microservices thinking.

Affordances and domain archetypes

Data quanta are the principal components of a domain and are described in terms of **affordances**. This is another new concept for many data warehouse practitioners. Affordances are simply defined as the relationships between the properties of a product and the capabilities of the agent (user) that determine how the product can be used. Affordances (or, perhaps more simply, functions) of data products include:

1. **Serve Data:** offer multimodal read-only access to immutable, bitemporal data via output data ports.

2. **Consume Data:** accept synchronous or asynchronous write or remote query; and support cross-port temporal synchronization via input data ports.

3. **Transform Data:** via programmatic or nonprogrammatic transformation of data and support time-variance.

4. **Compose Data:** by correlating or joining data with that of other products via computational set operations.

5. **Discover:** via APIs and CSI, allow users to discover, explore, understand, and trust the data product.

6. **Other functions:** Observe, govern, and manage product life cycles.

Based on the first three affordances, which often represent product-defining behaviors, data mesh proposes three domain data archetypes. Source-aligned (or native) domain data provides analytical data based directly on that generated by the domain's operational microservices. Aggregate domain data comes from multiple upstream (mostly source-aligned) domains. Consumer-aligned (or fit-for-purpose) domain data is aligned to the needs of one or more specific analytical use cases, with the data coming from source-aligned and/or aggregate domains. The latter two archetypes clearly depend on context mapping between the domains serving and receiving data to deliver results.

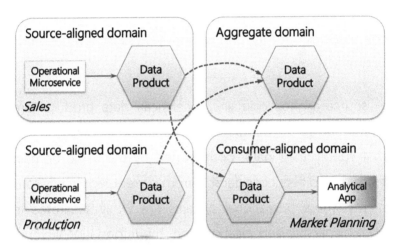

Figure 6.2: Domains and data products

Figure 6.2 is a simplified view of the relationships between domain archetypes. Source-aligned domains—sales and production—are each independently responsible for all the data in their own business functions, in both the operational microservices used and the analytical data products created. For simplicity, only one data product is shown in each domain; of course, there may be many in each. The data product in the aggregate domain consumes and combines data from both source domains. Market planning, a consumer-aligned domain, receives data from the aggregate domain and directly from the sales domain. In reality, there will be far more than four red dashed arrows, each representing the consumption of a data product. Each data-producing domain is responsible for the quality and completeness of the data it offers. Its product owners are charged with delighting *all* their potentially many customers by ensuring the ongoing completeness, quality, and responsiveness to new demands of their data products.

In source-aligned domains, (analytical) data products are paired and tightly integrated with operational microservices that supply their data, both owned by the same domain team. This differs considerably from current legacy environments where operational systems are firmly separated in both ownership and location from the informational world. Furthermore, they are most likely implemented as part of larger monolithic applications rather than microservices. Domains are clearly envisaged as spanning operational and analytical planes/environments (see Dehghani, 2020, Figure 7-3, for example), so extending the data mesh model beyond cloud-only implementations poses significant difficulties.

An additional challenge, of course, is to what extent do source and aggregate data product owners *really* care about downstream products. From the perspective of data warehousing, the difficulties in integrating and reconciling data from disparate sources are well-known. Separate business domains—each responsible for delivering data products within "independent bounded contexts"—prioritize quality and speed of delivery, agility in the face of constant change, and delivery of explicit business value. Very often, however, their developers operate under serious time and budget constraints. The outcome is well known: Downstream data consumers often end up at the bottom of the priority list.

Increase the number of dashed arrows in the above figure, and the picture will strongly resemble the spaghetti-like tangle of data transfers that predated and prompted data warehousing. Cynics may speak of data mess rather than data mesh. More kindly, we could compare the outputs to Kimball's 1990s independent data marts. The key question, therefore, is how data products can be combined to deliver cross-domain reconciled data versus unrelatable silos. Context mapping is thus absolutely central to data mesh.

Chapter IV of *Domain-Driven Design Reference* (Evans, 2015) offers advice on context mapping in strategic design. Eight distinct types of relationships between domains are identified: partnership, shared kernel, customer/supplier development, conformist, anticorruption layer, open-host service, published language, and separate ways. They clearly illustrate the challenges of context mapping in software product development. Evans further identifies the "big ball of mud" environments typical of legacy systems. Traditional data warehouse, data lake, and ETL pipeline developers are very familiar with many of these development situations. Only partnership fully meets data mesh's (and, indeed, data warehouse's) needs. It is exceedingly rare and difficult to achieve.

Data mesh has imported the concepts of domains and bounded contexts into the analytical world, promoting domains from settings for product development to business areas of responsibility for information. With data mesh's emphasis on decentralization and independent development, little consideration is given to the complexities of domain boundaries and context mapping identified by Evans, which are at the heart of creating consistent cross-domain and cross-data product aggregations[41]. This and the absence of an enterprise data model (see "*Federated computational governance*" below) present significant concerns for migration from a traditional data warehouse environment.

---

[41] For a deeper dive on these complexities within programming projects, see Brandolini, 2009. In fact, these challenges pale into insignificance in the data warehousing use case.

Structure of a data product

The concepts of immutable and bitemporal data in Serve Data—the first data product affordance above—will be very familiar to implementers of the enterprise data warehouse (EDW) layer of the DWC ADP. In immutable data, records are never deleted or changed; rather, inserts, updates, and deletes are appended to the dataset, with bitemporal metadata defining what action is occurring, thus generating and maintaining a historical record of the transitory and ever-changing data coming from operational systems and event streams. Downstream data marts may or may not adopt these structures depending on user needs. However, data products *must* adopt these approaches in all cases because there is no centralized EDW in which to create and manage a true, repeatable representation of history.

This immutable, bitemporal data structure is unusual in a service-oriented architecture. Pat Helland contrasts "data on the inside" of a service—representing the ever-changing now— with "data on the outside," which shows, by necessity, the point in time at which it was emitted (Helland, 2005). He concludes that the strengths of one stem from the weaknesses of the other. Traditional informational systems are populated through data-on-the-outside and expose a point-in-time view of data for user exploration. However, this approach is increasingly challenged as business demands a more real-time view, pushing our thinking back toward the encapsulated data-on-the-inside approach. Again, we face the original dilemma expressed in the timeliness/consistency axis of the IDEAL architecture information thinking space[42], for which there in no single, correct solution in every case.

By encapsulating all data into products, data mesh is choosing an approach that favors timeliness, implemented in a point-in-time structure designed for temporal consistency among events from a single source. It provides no support for cross-source consistency or reconciliation.

The operational/informational boundary

Data mesh claims to focus exclusively on the analytical world. Cloud data warehousing must consider BI and reporting as well, and the concept of data-as-a-product works here, too. However, consideration of the boundary between operational and informational systems raises awkward questions, especially when the operational environment consists of on-premises, legacy systems or integrated ERP or SaaS applications. Does domain ownership extend to these legacy data sources? And, if so, how do we construct a data product that

---

[42] See Volume I, chapter 3 for further details.

encapsulates all the legacy code and data, as well as the ETL feeding the informational environment?

Data warehouse implementers have long complained that they receive low-quality data from operational sources and struggle to get source errors rectified. This is, in part, an organizational problem. Extended domain and data product ownership could address it in a partnership relationship (as per Evans) between upstream and downstream systems mentioned in the previous section. However, it is difficult to envisage a functional solution without extending the bounded context of the domain into the operational environment. Indeed, the operational microservices shown _Figure 6.2_ above are clearly within the source-aligned domains. This would imply a high level of encapsulation in the operational environment—in essence, a shift to a microservices approach. This is clearly seen in Figure 13 of "Data Mesh Principles and Logical Architecture" (Dehghani, 2020). Furthermore, it implies that the ETL infrastructure found between the operational and informational environments must be dismantled and replaced with intra-domain pipelines.

This is a significant challenge for organizations with substantial legacy operational environments. Data mesh and its principles of domain ownership and data as a product are broadly framed as exclusively addressing the analytical environment—hence my parenthetical annotations in these sections' titles. However, this deeper dive into the workings of data products immediately reveals substantial and potentially costly impacts on the operational environment—especially in the case of legacy systems—of applying data mesh thinking to its full extent. Indeed, Dehghani's working example throughout her papers and book depicts a modern, relatively simple, web-based, and *fictional* enterprise. Examples of implementations and thinking to be found on the internet also focus almost exclusively on simple business scenarios in fully web-based implementations.

Note finally that the concept of data-as-a-product can be usefully applied within the operational environment and can offer support for the interoperability of such components, especially if based on a comprehensive semantic model. The breadth and depth of the data product concept as applied to the analytics environment is astounding, attractive, and likely enduring as vendors seek to benefit from software to enable it. We shall see...

A SELF-SERVE DATA PLATFORM

Of the four principal principles, the self-serve data platform is the most straight-forward, at least in terms of understanding and familiarity as a concept. It is frequently promoted in business intelligence and no-code software offerings. Its implementation, of course, is complex and potentially costly.

The purpose of this platform is simply to offset the challenges and costs of the highly distributed and cross-functional aspects of the previous two principles. Data mesh takes the high design and engineering skills in ETL, database design, and so on—today concentrated in the warehousing platform—and distributes and replicates them in multiple business domains. The data platform aims to diminish duplication of effort in each domain, avoid increased costs of operation, and reduce the potential for large-scale inconsistencies and incompatibilities across domains. In addition, it enables the use of more generalist design and engineering skills within the domains. This is achieved by extracting domain-agnostic capabilities, such as storage and database management, computing and transformation, and policy engines, out of each domain and moving them to a dedicated data platform team. The data platform in data mesh has the following features:

- Serves autonomous domain-oriented teams in building and using data products; data capture from disparate sources; and sharing the data products with the business.

- Manages autonomous and interoperable data products, including all aspects of data, metadata, code, policies, etc., encapsulated in a single unit.

- Provides a continuous, integrated platform of end-to-end operational and analytical capabilities.

- Is designed for use by a generalist majority by defining open conventions to promote interoperability between different technologies and reducing the number of skills and languages each specialist must master.

- Favors (new) decentralized technologies over existing centralized tooling such as orchestration, catalogs, warehouse schema, resource allocation, and so on.

- Supports domain-agnostic platform capabilities, as well as enabling domain-specific data modeling, processing, and sharing capabilities.

The data platform aims to be self-serve for all users of the mesh. This platform is not just for data product developers, but also for data product owners and users. Each of these and other personae has specific needs. A developer, for example, needs support throughout the lifecycle of the product—development, test, deployment, and maintenance, as well as ensuring quality and security. The role of the platform is to provide the capabilities—both domain-agnostic and cross-functional—to allow the developer to perform all the above tasks without knowing the underlying technical infrastructure. Similarly, the platform must provide function for users to discover, access, compose, understand, analyze, and explore the data autonomously and without friction.

The implementation challenge for a data platform is that, as of this writing, you have to build it largely from scratch, although Dehghani's description is sufficient to conceive of a product-based solution[43]. The data mesh implementations described on the web are notable for their ingenuity and roll-your-own nature. The adoption of data mesh appears to be highest among organizations with substantial open-source infrastructure development skills. They are often cloud native and thus can avoid the complexities that on-premises, legacy operational systems present.

FEDERATED COMPUTATIONAL GOVERNANCE

Compared to the other data warehousing approaches discussed so far, data mesh places a much stronger emphasis on governance. This is a welcome development in thinking: Good governance is central to successful value delivery in data warehousing but is often vestigial or even missing entirely in technology-driven implementations.

---

[43] Nextdata was founded in 2022 by Zhamak Dehghani to develop such a product. As of March 2024, it is not yet available. www.nextdata.com

Of course, data mesh, with its highly distributed data architecture and ownership model, as well as data as a product, cries out for a far higher level of governance and management than more centralized approaches. Data mesh addresses this with a federated governance model to assure that the mesh of independently created and maintained products is of the highest quality. In contrast to prior, manual governance processes, data mesh proposes—as far as possible—a rules-based, computational approach to governance, embedded in the data platform and products. Overlaid on this is a centralization only of global decisions that affect the broader ecosystem, drive interoperability, and enable discovery and composition of data products. This strategy is designed to embrace an environment in constant change and to be able to respond rapidly to such change.

Ongoing, localized responsibility for governance resides with domain and platform component owners, who can react with speed and agility to changes in the environment. This is facilitated by operationalizing the governance policies, standards, and rules into the operation of the platform via systems thinking elements, such as leverage points and feedback loops, to create a state of dynamic governance equilibrium. For example, rather than trying to limit up-front the creation of duplicate data products, the system promotes successful, quality data products to businesspeople at the expense of less popular, poorer quality ones that "die on the vine." Such computational governance is, of course, easier to describe than to implement with current tooling. It is a worthwhile goal, but lacking a comprehensive self-serve data platform product, this embedded, rule-based, computational approach is challenging to deliver.

The definition of, and agreement on, governance policies, standards, and rules are the function of an overarching organization. This is seen as a federation of domain representatives and data product owners, working with specialists in interoperability, security, and platform function. At this level, we see standardization of data product syntactical and semantic modeling, as well as of shared metadata elements and formats. Identification of rules for domain boundary setting and associated data products also occurs in the federated governance team.

A traditional data warehousing practitioner might also expect to see responsibility here for an overarching enterprise data model (EDM) to allow and ensure interoperability between data products from different domains. Data mesh does not oblige; a centralized EDM does not feature! In fact, relational schemata with facts and dimensions or foreign relationships are also dismissed as creating "tight and fragile" links between data products. Data mesh strongly prefers "loose coupling" between products, to minimize the bottle-necks of centralized synchronization points.

Instead of an explicit definition of relationships between data in products, data mesh proposes a **distributed type system** (set of schemata[44]), where each data product independently owns and controls its own schema. Loose coupling allows one data product to use and refer to other products' schemata and data and use the mappings from one data product to its neighboring ones to identify what is relatable and how. This implies that data product owners must not just be aware of related data in other products but also be motivated to enable data users to easily build meaningful relationships.

This pushes cross-product data modeling down to the users of the system; essentially a reversion to the schema-on-read philosophy of early data lakes. This approach does not engender confidence in the interoperability of data products. Furthermore, it may present practical challenges in a range of important areas where a common, shared data model is useful, including defining the top-level data catalog / business glossary; auto-classification of data; enterprise-level privacy, sovereignty, and security rules; and data quality, lineage, and lifecycle management.

---

[44] Schemata is the plural of schema.

Principles and practices summary

The above principles constitute deeply thoughtful and highly innovative thinking about the needs for and constraints on the delivery of analytical and informational needs in the modern world of ubiquitous, distributed data and rapidly evolving business needs, often framed around real-time decision making and action taking. These principles are defined in Dehghani's seminal work (Dehghani, 2019, 2020, 2022). Another comprehensive source of information is "Data Mesh Architecture: Data Mesh from an Engineering Perspective" (Christ et al, 2022). We see that data mesh is driven entirely by a world view that has emerged from highly volatile, cloud-native, microservices- and data-centric businesses.

It may be that such an architectural approach is the only one capable of supporting such environments, although this so far remains unproven. However, the approach also raises significant concerns of a practical nature, particularly for organizations that come from a clicks-and-mortar background and with a significant level of legacy IT systems. As we next describe the data mesh ADP, it is immediately obvious that this pattern differs significantly from those defined thus far.

DATA MESH ADP

Data mesh is built upon data products rather than data stores or databases, as shown in the data mesh ADP, *Figure 6.3* below.

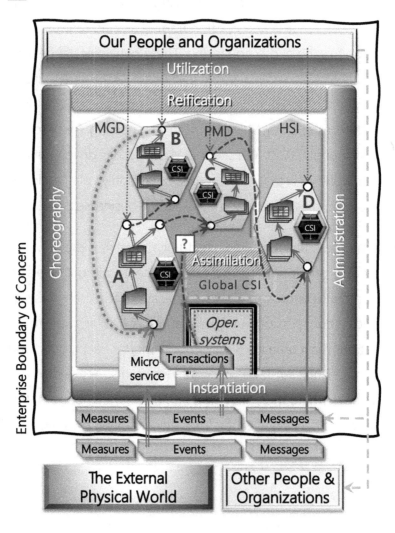

Figure 6.3: ADP: Data mesh

All data stores are now encapsulated into higher level data products (mauve hexagons, labeled **A**-**D**), together with supporting process/code (maroon double arrows) and CSI. Each data product can have multiple input and output ports (the small white circles). Data product **A** is paired with a microservice that creates business transaction data based on, for example, external events (blue double arrow). It is thus owned by a source-aligned domain and implemented entirely in the cloud. Domains, as organizational concepts, are not shown in the ADP.

As described in *"A self-serve data platform,"* all embedded function, CSI, and data structures, as well as data product features, are constructed with the support of the infrastructure provided by the data platform. In the ADP, this is represented by the fully functional process components of instantiation, choreography, administration, and utilization. Note, however, that much of this function is implemented within the data products, supported by the data platform.

Assimilation is shown cross-hatched; its function is limited in data mesh as a result of the restricted support for any form of enterprise model or cross-source reconciliation. However, it has a role in the creation and management of global CSI.

Reification, or data virtualization, is also shown as limited in function for two reasons. The first is that data mesh mentions data virtualization only as an **antipattern**: "exposing analytical data directly from the operational database[45]." The second is that reification also requires some form of enterprise model to allow data in different formats and locations to be found, translated into business-friendly form, and joined as needed.

Both these functional limitations echo the significant concern about the absence of any overarching semantic model in data mesh. A cynic might rename the concept "data mush"! As a result, access to data products is only possible at an individual, stand-alone level from utilization. In addition, data input to data products (solid blue arrow) and transfer between data products (maroon, dashed arrows) are defined as one-to-one, source-target mappings. Of course, in real-life, there will be many mappings to be defined and managed between data product owners and source data suppliers in pair-wise agreements between domains. On a more positive note, these agreements offer a perfect solution to implementing reverse flows of data (the blue, dashed, highlighted arrow between data products **B** and **A**).

Data products in data mesh give no consideration as to whether the data/information they contain is classed as MGD, PMD, or HSI. However, the pillars are shown as a

---

[45] This would certainly **not** be considered an antipattern in data fabric.

reminder to implementers of this pattern that such typing should be kept in mind. It forms the basis for decisions on data storage technologies within the data products.

Special attention must be paid to on-premises, legacy, operational sources of data in cloud data warehousing solutions. In the case of data mesh, early indications are not promising. The green dotted box in *Figure 6.3* represents legacy operational systems and here is surrounded by a heavy double, black physical storage boundary. Business transactions are, of course, created by such systems from events (the dashed, double, blue arrow) and other sources. These systems differ from the adjacent microservice, typically being large, monolithic systems, on-premises and unaligned to the domain structure proposed by data mesh.

So, how are these transactions ingested into the analytical environment? Data mesh provides no obvious answer. We speculate here that an aggregate domain negotiates a feed (red, dashed, highlighted, and annotated ?) into data product **C** from the legacy operational system. In terms of governance, this differs significantly from the case for data product **A**, which is in a source-aligned domain that owns both the data product and the microservice that supplies its data. In addition, in the real world, there will exist a multitude of such "?" feeds, in a likely return to the data sourcing "rats' nest" that preceded data warehousing.

DATA MESH ADP—CONCLUSIONS

This analysis, based closely on the extensive work of the inventor of data mesh, Zhamak Dehghani, allows us to summarize the strengths and weaknesses of the data mesh ADP and come to some high-level conclusions about its value and applicability to real-life situations.

PROS OF THE DATA MESH ADP

- **Business domains are a more "natural" decomposition axis of responsibility for data.**

  Traditional data warehousing patterns tend to lead to responsibility for data governance being aligned to the technology layers of the architecture. This is especially detrimental in the case of a centralized EDW or lake. Data mesh entirely adopts a business domain approach for governance, in addition to completely avoiding centralization of data and function.

- **Data as a product focuses on business domains taking responsibility for their data delighting customers.**

  A fully product-centric approach to data sees data products as first-class citizens and lifts our sights up from individual and often poorly managed data sets. In contrast, data products contain everything needed to create, discover, understand, and use the embedded data. Product owners take responsibility for the continued quality and evolution of their products, such that their clients can completely trust the data they receive.

- **Business-centric design and development of data-as-a-product (BI/analytics) deliverables.**

  Business domain driven design and product thinking are particularly appropriate for BI and analytics deliverables, which are consequently sharply focused on real and well-defined business requirements.

- **Avoids development bottlenecks as a consequence of a lack of domain knowledge in centralized data delivery teams, such as enterprise modeling, ETL, and so on.**

  Where central teams are technology oriented, handovers to and from business-oriented source and target teams can be slow and unwieldy. Business domain orientation across the full stack avoids the resulting bottlenecks in development and maintenance, which is most often the result of business-driven change.

- **Centralized data governance bottlenecks are removed, with federated, rules-driven governance being embedded in the computational infrastructure, automating day-to-day data governance activities.**

A new approach to data governance replaces up-front standards definition and enforcement with continuous, automated, rules-based governance applied at runtime. Only truly global governance decisions are centralized and form the foundation for a largely federated and 24/7 automated governance environment.

Cons of the data mesh ADP

- Despite Dehghani's strong conceptual guidance and architecture, there exist multiple, divergent, low-level, implementation-focused definitions of data mesh.

  Possibly as a result of the novelty of the concepts (to the informational world, at least), with their focus on modern or emerging software development techniques, a broad, diverse community of developers and start-up vendors has emerged. The result is that a wide variety of subtly different, and sometimes widely divergent, interpretations and implementation approaches have emerged. At the extreme, this includes data mesh descriptions that include data warehouses as "data products," contrary to data mesh's rejection of such centralized structures.

- Significant in-house development effort is currently required to implement data mesh.

Like data warehouse, data mesh is *not* a product and never will be. Product support in certain areas is needed and is emerging, although this is slow, given the novelty of some of the underpinning concepts. The result is that, as of this writing, many implementations are hand crafted, based on internal and innovative development, and focused on specific business needs and situations.

This is beginning to change, albeit slowly. Nextdata, for example, promises "a data-mesh-native toolset built to meet the challenge of decentralizing data at scale."

- **Context-setting information (metadata) standards, tools, and methods are lacking or poorly supported.**

  This is the same as the first two issues listed for data fabric in *"Cons of the data fabric ADP,"* although the focus moves from the centralized connected knowledge graph promoted there to the federated, encapsulated implementation envisaged in data mesh. The current state of standards in metadata sharing and the immature support for distributed metadata heavily impact the delivery of the more advanced metadata facilities required for a fully mature data mesh.

- **Reconciliation of data across sources (as seen in EDW and MDM) is a very particular need of mature businesses** that is not addressed in domain driven design and does not appear to have been considered in data mesh.

The focus of data mesh on business domain driven design, combined with an aversion to centralization in any form, presents a significant challenge for cross-functional data integration. Pairwise, negotiated data aggregation, as proposed, likely leads to an unmanageable, *ad hoc*, multi-point, spaghetti environment.

- **Spreading development resources across multiple domains may lead to inefficiency and skills dilution.**

Data mesh proposes an extensive, self-serve data and infrastructure platform to reduce the development skills needed within each domain and push technical specialization down to that platform. However, for now, such platform support is embryonic and significant technical skills will be required in every domain.

- **Decentralization and federation are known to cause significant disruption in organizations with immature data governance and/or systems management.**

Most data delivery and informational systems organizations today have operated in hierarchical and/or centralized fashions since their inception decades ago. Changing this way of working can be a big ask. Where federated approaches have been tried (typically in cloud-based operational environments), failures are closely cor-related with low governance or systems management maturity. See, for example, "Is Data Mesh right for your organisation?" (Hyperight, 2021).

DATA MESH ADP: IS IT YOUR DESTINATION?

Data mesh has certainly attracted significant attention in the data warehousing and analytics community since its launch in 2019. However, as will be clear from the preceding sec-tions, it starts from a very different mindset than the other patterns explored here. As a concept, it shuns many tradi-tional assumptions, especially centralization—of data and governance—and opts for a strongly federated and business domain-driven approach.

To answer the question posed in the title above, we must focus on the features described in the "*Data mesh ADP*" sec-tion and the accompanying picture. At this level, data mesh leaves many implementation options open and, given the relative immaturity of available supporting software, many implementers are building their own platforms. Furthermore, we must beware of vendors who are conflating aspects of fabric or lakehouse with data mesh to suit their own offer-ings. So, what is your journey and how could you best un-dertake it?

The starting gate

Starting a data mesh journey from anywhere other than a fully cloud-based operational and informational environment seems unrealistic. Migrating from an existing on-premises data warehouse to data mesh would be a major undertaking, both in terms of the warehouse itself and the existing ETL feeds into this warehouse. Data mesh, as currently defined, does not address ingestion of the types of data feeds typically found in on-premises data warehouses.

So, the starting point for a data mesh journey is a cloud-based analytical environment. If your environment conforms to the DWC/cn architectural design pattern, a cloud-based lake + warehouse pseudo-ADP, or the data lakehouse ADP, careful consideration of your existing reconciliation approach and potential requirements is strongly recommended, given data mesh's limited support for data reconciliation needs.

That leaves as the most viable starting point a cloud-based, highly siloed analytical environment, where analytical needs are largely based on functionally aligned data, allowing the business domain concept to be applied from source all the way to target. If there is any existing cross-functional integration or reconciliation, it should be largely confined to localized and well-understood cases.

The journey

The journey to data mesh will likely consist of two parallel paths. On the first of these is the development of software to deliver the minimum data platform components. Although some vendors are offering data mesh solutions, none cover the full scope of what is required, and many are extremely limited, focusing on only one aspect of what is needed for a full implementation. Indeed, some vendors redefine or de-scope what data mesh is, an approach that should give potential clients pause for thought.

Irrespective of these considerations, it would be advisable to have skilled and experienced open-source, cloud developers on board to build new or extend existing software components to create the data platform and interfaces required. The technical debt implications of such an approach must be carefully considered.

The second path will entail ramping up skills across the organization to deal with the decentralized and federated governance environment that data mesh demands. New data product owner roles will need to be launched and frameworks designed to support collaborative work between data suppliers and customers. The required organizational change management should not be underestimated.

The destination

A complete realization of all aspects of data mesh as described by Dehghani in her seminal papers and book—and on which the analysis in this chapter is based—may be beyond the reach of many mainstream enterprises. This conclusion is derived from both organizational and IT considerations.

Data mesh's pivot toward federated and decentralized management of data delivery and governance is likely to pose significant challenges to many traditional organizations. Although widely promoted by consultants in organizational design and change management, the experience of real-life attempts to fully adopt these principles has often proven challenging. The data mesh approach demands considerable maturity in these areas across the entire organization.

IT faces additional challenges. In addition to adopting the federated paradigms above and taking on board novel data-as-a-product concepts and practices, IT will, in many cases, need to undertake the development of infrastructure that should ideally be provided by software products, especially in the coming years as vendors develop and evolve their offerings. Existing, traditional data warehousing teams are unlikely to have the necessary skills for such work. Early infrastructure implementers will also need to consider later possible migration costs to product solutions.

Taking the above *caveats* into account, the destination for a data mesh ADP journey beginning now is far from clear. If you consider that you have the business support and awareness, as well as the organizational and IT skills and experience required, extensive prototyping and pilot implementations over the first few years would be well advised. Early migration of an existing data warehousing ADP to a fully-fledged data mesh is likely an extremely high-risk approach.

TAKEAWAYS

- Data mesh was first introduced in 2019 by Thoughtworks consultant and now founder and CEO of Nextdata, Zhamak Dehghani, as a novel, alternative approach to delivering analytics and avoiding the problems associated with monolithic, centralized, and domain-agnostic data lakes (and warehouses).

- Although the definitions and descriptions of data lake and warehouse used by Dehghani are flawed in many aspects, the problems listed are well-described and generally accepted by the industry.

- Three architecture failure modes of the prior approaches to data lakes / warehouses are listed: (i) a centralized, monolithic platform supports neither proliferation of data sets nor innovation, (ii) rework of a full data pipeline is required for the smallest changes in business needs, and (iii) ownership of different parts of the information creation process is siloed and hyper-specialized.

- Four principles underpin data mesh:

  o Domain ownership of (analytical) data

  o (Analytical) data as a product

  o A self-serve data platform

  o Federated computational governance

- Evans' principles of domain-driven design have been adapted and expanded to encompass the development of analytical systems, with business domain ownership extending along the full length of the data pipelines and built upon self-describing, encapsulated data products architected according to service-oriented practices.

- A platform-based approach is adopted by data mesh to insulate business domain owners and developers from the technicalities of data product design, delivery, and governance. This further supports a move from manual governance to a rules-based, computational approach.

- A significant concern from a traditional data warehousing viewpoint with this domain-oriented, data product approach is the apparent lack of any viable, controlled method of reconciling data across data products and domains. Data mesh proposes this be done solely through binary producer-consumer negotiations.

- The lack of an enterprise data model also has significant impacts on many aspects of metadata/CSI management and use.

- The data mesh ADP differs significantly from other data warehousing ADPs previously described, with a focus on data products rather than on the datasets and databases that are foundational in the DWC and data lakehouse ADPs, and the centralized, automated data management of the data fabric ADP.

- Data mesh is a singularly cloud-focused approach. Little or no consideration seems to have been given to the well-known and real challenges of obtaining and reconciling data from legacy, on-premises environments.

- As a consequence, a cloud-based environment containing both operational apps and largely siloed analytics is likely the only feasible starting point for the journey to the data mesh ADP.

- This journey will require significant infrastructure software development by skilled cloud / open-source engineers in the early stages. Extensive, prior experience of decentralized/federated delivery and governance environments is highly desirable.

- The above considerations make the destination for an early data mesh ADP journey unclear. Even with adequate organizational and IT skills and experience, extensive prototyping and pilot implementations over the first few years would be well advised. Early migration of an existing data warehousing ADP to a fully-fledged data mesh is likely an extremely high-risk program.

Chapter 7

Journey's End

If all difficulties were known at the outset of a long journey,
most of us would never start out at all.

Dan Rather

It has certainly been a long journey. And tortuous, too. From the mainframe-based data warehouses of the 1980s to the various cloud-centric patterns explored here, we have surely started out and traveled far. The path has taken us to destinations both exotic and mundane. We have learned much. But I suspect the journey is far from over and may, in truth, be never ending.

In this second and final part of the *Cloud Data Warehousing* series, we explored some more modern architectural thinking, but our main focus has been a deep dive into all the architectural design patterns that have emerged over nearly forty years of data warehousing. And now, in the final chapter, we'll assess which of the three emergent cloud-centric

ADPs is likely to best meet your circumstances and needs. The brief answer is, of course, a consultant's "it depends!"

But first, we look at one major analyst/consultant firm's view.

GARTNER'S HYPE CYCLE FOR DATA MANAGEMENT

The Gartner Hype Cycle for Data Management, 2023 (Rosenbaum, 2023) covers many of the key topics discussed here as part of a comprehensive review of evolving data management matters. *Figure 7.1*, adapted from the more comprehensive figure in this document[46], shows Gartner's positioning of four ADPs—data lake, data fabric, data mesh, and data lakehouse. Data warehouse, whether cloud or otherwise, is omitted, perhaps being too far to the right on the plateau of productivity ☺ . Other components of these patterns, such as data product, active metadata management, and knowledge graphs, are also discussed in the full report. The definitions used by Gartner may differ from those defined by the ADPs here. However, at the higher levels discussed here, these differences have limited significance.

---

[46] As of this writing, the full report is available from at www.tamr.com/resources/gartner-hype-cycle-for-data-management-2023.

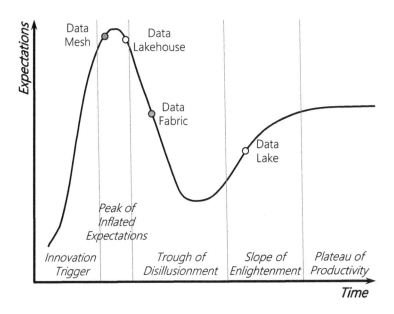

Figure 7.1: Hype cycle for cloud data warehousing

The categories on the time axis of the hype cycle are well known and largely self-explanatory.

Predictably, data lake is shown furthest along the evolutionary path. More surprising, perhaps, is the judgment (shown by the color of the dot) that the plateau of productivity is still 2-5 years out, given data lake's long history. However, the obstacles are those we previously identified—a severe lack of metadata and limitations in the design and governance of the data stores included.

Data fabric—the concept promoted by Gartner—although plunging into the trough of disillusionment, is shown as the next furthest traveled on the evolutionary journey and rated as transformational. However, it is still seen as 5-10 years from maturity. The obstacles discussed align closely with those we saw in *"Cons of the data fabric ADP"* relating to active metadata management maturity, as well as the differing and immature metadata standards across the industry.

Data lakehouse and data mesh are both to be found at the peak of inflated expectations, although Gartner's judgments on them differ considerably. Lakehouse is seen to be 2-5 years from the plateau, and the fastest moving pattern. This reflects the relative maturity of, and vendor support for, many of the underlying technologies. Obstacles noted include a divergence of vendor focus areas on either the warehouse or analytics aims of the approach, as well as the challenge of complex warehouse scenarios.

Perhaps the most surprising aspect of the analysis relates to data mesh, defined by Gartner as an evolving "data management approach". The report asserts that, despite its rapid growth in hype (moving from innovation trigger in 2022 to peak of inflated expectations in 2023), it is likely to be obsolete before it reaches the plateau (the red dot). This is based on the likelihood that its core capabilities are likely to be subsumed into data fabric. Of interest also is the introduction of data product—a key component of data mesh—in the innovation trigger phase as transformational and with a time to plateau of 2-5 years in the full report (Rosenbaum, 2023). Gartner clearly sees data-as-a-product as having a life beyond data mesh.

COMPARING THE CLOUD-FOCUSED ADPs

In this volume, we have explored four cloud data warehousing ADPs: DWC/cn, data lakehouse, data fabric, and data mesh. Each has, of course, its strengths and weaknesses, reflecting where its proponents place importance. These have been discussed in the pros and cons sections of the last three chapters, from which you should have reached a view on which of these are important in your organization.

As a final review of the four patterns, let's pose the same question for each: "Are you ready to build one?" In each case, we assume the optimal starting gate explicitly identified earlier for the lakehouse, fabric, and mesh ADPs and implied for DWC/cn.

ARE YOU READY TO BUILD A DWC/CN?

The most likely starting point for this ADP is the desire to migrate from an existing on-premises data warehouse implementation (DWC/op) to the cloud, as part of a larger shift of all new development to the cloud. Key questions are:

- Is your existing DWC/op successful in terms of business satisfaction and IT design and delivery?

- Are you comfortable with a centralized data warehouse and centralized governance and development?

- Are you happy to see a perhaps lengthy migration of all on-premises operational systems to the cloud or that some of these systems remain permanently on premises?

- Does your existing data warehouse include substantial and complex computation, perhaps dependent on a proprietary vendor database or ETL implementation?

- Are your BI/reporting and analytic needs relatively distinct and separate?

If you replied in the affirmative to most of the above questions, the DWC/cn ADP is likely to be a good choice for you.

DWC/cn is the "obvious" migration path for traditional data warehousing to the cloud. That brings with it a set of beliefs around the foundational principles of data warehousing and architectural approaches to data warehouse design. As a result, it may be less suited to advanced analytic and machine learning needs (depending on your choice of product vendor), which may need separate implementation.

ARE YOU READY TO BUILD A DATA LAKEHOUSE?

Starting from a data lake with embedded data warehouse functionality (see "*Lake + warehouse pseudo-ADP*"), the key questions to answer are:

- Do you have or need a (single) data lake that truly embeds your traditional data warehousing needs?

- Are you copying or deriving vast quantities of data within your lake?

- Do you need to combine large quantities of data for machine learning and reporting across PMD and MGD/HSI?

- Has your information preparation environment become extremely complex and difficult to manage?

- Are you committed to a cloud solution for all your informational needs?

If you answered "yes" to the majority of these questions, the data lakehouse ADP may be your preferred choice.

Recalling that data lakehouse combines the best (and worst) of data lake and warehouse, there are some important *caveats* to consider. You will likely require strong technical skills in open-source development. Lakehouse software is still relatively immature, so workarounds will be required, especially for on-premises sources. The principles of data warehousing must still be applied (far beyond what is normally encountered in a data lake), including enterprise level modeling, reconciliation of data across multiple sources, and data governance at an enterprise level.

ARE YOU READY TO BUILD A DATA FABRIC?

Starting from a logical data warehouse ADP or, less ideally, a DWC/op or DWC/cn, you should ask the following questions:

- How far have you progressed toward a logical data warehouse with a centralized DWC ADP either on premises or in the cloud?

- Are you comfortable with your existing data warehousing approach and feel it worthwhile to build on existing investments?

- How good or complete is your metadata / context-setting information (CSI) management environment?

- Do you have the organization and effective working methods for collecting CSI that could be automated?

- Have you investigated, piloted, or implemented data virtualization tools?

If you answered positively to the majority of these questions, you are in a good place to begin weaving a data fabric, given that a good LDW is the basis of data fabric and CSI is a vital foundation.

Recalling that the essence of data fabric is the integration and automation of information preparation and access, you should keep in mind that data fabric software is still immature in certain areas, so some workarounds will be required. Consider also that vendors are currently offering incomplete, competing, or incompatible solutions, and that metadata standards and sharing remain a significant challenge in the industry.

ARE YOU READY TO BUILD A DATA MESH?

With the starting condition being an existing fully cloud-based and mostly siloed operational and informational environment, the following questions are key:

- Have you implemented microservices in your operational or other data sources?

- Have you adopted domain-driven design (DDD) anywhere in your organization?

- How skilled are you in microservices, Agile development, and DDD approaches?

- How willing is your data team to adopt and adapt these approaches?

- How mature is your organization in decentralized or federated operation and decision making?

- Is consolidated/reconciled data between reporting and analytics mostly unimportant to your organization?

Positive answers to a majority of these questions suggests you may be in a good place to begin weaving a data mesh.

Keep in mind that data mesh demands very different organization and governance approaches that require significant redesign for agility, as well as decentralization of governance and development. Furthermore, the software currently available for data mesh is very immature, so significant bespoke infrastructure development will be required.

Finally, be aware that a true enterprise data warehouse is not formally included in the original data mesh specification (although some vendors include it) and that Gartner's view is that data mesh will be subsumed into data fabric.

WHAT ABOUT MIX AND MATCH?

Our approach in this series has focused on "architectural purity", defining clearly and concisely the different patterns of data warehousing we've seen over the years. We've thus ended up with four relatively distinct ADPs for cloud data warehousing, each with its own strengths and weaknesses.

In the real world, of course, vendors propose their own definitions, often more aligned with their product sets than underpinning architectural truths. Implementers, too, adopt the most suitable aspects of different ADPs, depending on business priorities, historical solutions, and even personal preferences. The reality is that there are few green-field situations anymore, and architects must define their modern solutions within the constraints of often challenging brown-field sites.

Data architecture is a continuously evolving practice that may—and probably must—adopt principles and features from all of today's recognized ADPs and should be ready to adjust those for future, as yet unseen, patterns. So, mix and match is a fact.

Across the market, a number of trends in mix and match are clear as of this writing. The term *data lakehouse* is increasingly used to cover both the DWC/cn and data lakehouse ADPs defined here. Inmon's support for the term (see "*Evolving the data lakehouse concept*") has likely been a driver in this trend, despite his uncommon definition of the lakehouse structure. With storage technology converging on open storage formats built on object stores, the difference between these two patterns largely reduces to one of emphasis on data governance, in which area DWC/cn historically has a stronger position.

Data fabric and data mesh are also increasingly being conflated; after all, in common usage, *mesh* and *fabric* mean much the same thing. However, such conflation is false. Although both ADPs are decentralized, data mesh starts from a very different set of governance principles that **demand** decentralization and federation, while data fabric accepts *ad hoc* decentralization largely as a given. However, it is likely that some of the governance and data product thinking of data mesh could conceivably be implemented—at least in part—on the technical foundation of data fabric.

Data lakehouse and DWC/cn can certainly be extended by data fabric to allow data from beyond the physically centralized store to be incorporated into users' query results. And both can surely benefit from the active metadata thinking of data fabric.

Suggestions by some consultants and vendors that DWC/cn or lakehouse can be augmented by data mesh must, however, be treated with considerable caution. Data mesh, as originally defined, vehemently opposes any forms of centralized data warehouse stores, preferring instead domain-oriented data products as the basic architectural construct.

In Conclusion

We began this series by defining the first and fundamental purpose of cloud data warehousing as the cloud-based *delivery of consistent, integrated, timely, quality, useful, and usable data primarily to business users.* This definition was deliberately chosen to emphasize the continuity of thought stretching from the first data warehouses of the 1980s to the lakehouses, fabrics, and meshes of today. The aim was to provide a firm architectural foundation for an exploration of the currently popular—and often confusing—solutions offered by the market today to meet the above purpose.

Accepting DWC/cn as the logical and simplest migration of traditional on-premises thinking and methods to the cloud, we are left with the three emergent ADPs—data lakehouse, data fabric, and data mesh—as the focus of this section.

These new architectural patterns offer novel and valuable considerations and lessons for data warehousing. While data fabric and data lakehouse primarily address technology issues and opportunities, data mesh puts its focus firmly on development organization challenges. All are, however, primarily technology driven approaches.

All three present considerable challenges to early implementation. The required software is immature to varying degrees and thinking about governance and development methods still inadequate. Data lakehouse and mesh, in particular, demand a skilled and mature IT environment.

None address the basic challenge of decision-making support—to ensure information leads to better human decisions and actions—to any greater degree than prior approaches. (Nor, indeed, does the move to cloud data warehousing!) By largely ignoring the people thinking space of the conceptual, IDEAL architecture described in Volume I, they contribute to the long-standing myth that collecting ever more data leads directly and inevitably to better decision making. The deconstruction of that myth, presented at length in *Business unIntelligence* (Devlin, 2013), still stands.

In his extensive 2024 new year review (Frisendal, 2024) of how we are doing in data management—in the broadest sense of both words—author and consultant, Thomas Frisendal, declares: "you can apply lots and lots of engineering tools, but the job will only be done if you know the subjects of the business domains, know the business concerns, and solve the issues together with the businesspeople in federated scenarios." The comment perfectly captures my central issue with all three cloud data warehousing patterns: a focus on technology to the exclusion of business outcomes of data warehousing—insightful decisions and knowledgeable actions, delivered repeatably, easily, and elegantly.

AND FINALLY...

Written in 1985, my final paragraph of the internal IBM pro-
posal for a data warehouse read: "We believe the proposed
architecture is an essential prerequisite to delivering business
information in a fast, consistent, and controlled manner and
to cope with the ever-changing business demands and
productivity pressures of this decade and the next." Almost
four decades later, the belief remains valid, although the
scope of what we demand from business information has
vastly expanded from the simple reporting and direct query-
ing we envisaged at the time. Sadly, the "fast, consistent, and
controlled" delivery of business information remains as challenging now as it did then, despite the many orders of mag-
nitude of increased computing power seen in the interim.

And from this distance, the data and decisions of the 1980s
seem insignificant, inconsequential. Forty years ago, business
data was little more than simple sales numbers and call detail
records. Now, we cache vast swathes of information spanning from the frontiers of space to the intimacies of human
behavior. In the 1980s, our decisions perhaps impacted a
salesperson's commission. Today, we seek to influence our
children's purchases and often end up driving them to des-
pair. We put the fate of humanity and, indeed, the entire
planet, in the virtual hands of our decision-making algorithms and our generative artificial (so-called) intelligence. All

based on data we know to be poorly governed, inconsistent, low quality, biased, increasingly faked. What could possibly go wrong?

Although our focus throughout these two volumes has been architectural and technical, aimed at helping IT to decide how to deliver cloud data warehousing, a far deeper and more important topic—for the whole organization—looms. What outcomes do we desire from cloud data warehousing? What do we mean by improved decision making? Which decisions should we be improving? How trustworthy is the information that supports such decisions?

I sincerely hope that these two volumes may help you reach your cloud data warehousing destination. More importantly, I pray that these closing paragraphs may cause you to pause on your journey. To consider what outcomes you and your organization hope to achieve. To step beyond the technology choices, to put aside the forty years of architectural wisdom shared here and ponder (as I do): At the end of my career in data warehousing, for what would I wish to be remembered? What difference in the *real* world did I make?

I opened both volumes of this series with Joni Mitchell's poetic depiction of clouds as "rows and flows of angel hair," from her song "Both Sides Now," amazingly penned as a 23-year-old in 1966. The arc of the song led her to ponder love's disappointments and life's vicissitudes, so it seems unavoidable to close with her beautiful, parting words:

> *But now old friends are acting strange*
> *They shake their heads, they say I've changed*
> *Well something's lost, but something's gained*
> *In living every day.*
>
> *I've looked at life from both sides now*
> *From win and lose and still somehow*
> *It's life's illusions I recall*
> *I really don't know life at all.*

References

Ackoff, R. L., "From data to wisdom", 1989, Journal of Applied Systems Analysis, Volume 15, pp. 3-9

Anderson, Carl, *Creating a Data-Driven Organization*, 2015, O'Reilly Media, CA, learning.oreilly.com/library/view/creating-a-data-driven/9781491916902/ [accessed 10 August 2023]

Armbrust, M., Gowda, B., Tavakoli-Shiraji, A., Xin, R., Zaharia, M., & Ghodsi, A., "Frequently Asked Questions About the Data Lakehouse", 2021, www.databricks.com/blog/2021/08/30/frequently-asked-questions-about-the-data-lakehouse.html [accessed 6 October 2023]

Avidon, E., "BI adoption poised to break through barrier – finally", 2023, TechTarget, www.techtarget.com/searchbusinessanalytics/news/365530077/BI-adoption-poised-to-break-through-barrier-finally [accessed 2 August 2023]

Baer, T., "Data Lakehouse open source market landscape", 2023, dbInsight LLC, www.dbinsight.io/form-data-lakehouse-open-source-market-landscape [accessed 15 October 2023]

Berkun, S., "The Dangers of Faith In Data", 2013, Blog, scottberkun.com/2013/danger-of-faith-in-data/ [accessed 10 August 2023]

Beyer, M. A., "Data Fabric Architecture is Key to Modernizing Data Management and Integration", 2021, Gartner Insights, www.gartner.com/smarterwithgartner/data-fabric-architecture-is-key-to-modernizing-data-management-and-integration [accessed 31 October 2023]

Blumauer, A., "Introduction to Knowledge Graphs and Semantic AI", 2019, Slideshare, www.slideshare.net/semwebcompany/introduction-to-knowledge-graphs-and-semantic-ai [accessed 15 November 2023]

Brandolini, A., "Strategic Domain Driven Design with Context Mapping", 2009, InfoQ, www.infoq.com/articles/ddd-contextmapping/ [accessed 26 November 2023]

Brynjolfsson, E., "The Turing Trap: The Promise & Peril of Human-Like Artificial Intelligence", 2022, Stanford Digital Economy Lab, digitaleconomy.stanford.edu/news/the-turing-trap-the-promise-peril-of-human-like-artificial-intelligence/ [accessed 18 February 2024]

Christ, J., Visengeriyeva, L., & Harrer, S., "Data Mesh Architecture: Data Mesh from an Engineering Perspective", 2022, Innoq, www.datamesh-architecture.com [accessed 11 February 2024]

Dehghani, Z., "How to Move Beyond a Monolithic Data Lake to a Distributed Data Mesh", 2019, martinfowler.com/articles/data-monolith-to-mesh.html [accessed 17 November 2023]

Dehghani, Z., "Data Mesh Principles and Logical Architecture", 2020, martinfowler.com/articles/data-mesh-principles.html, [accessed 17 November 2023]

Dehghani, Z., *Data Mesh, Delivering Data-Driven Value at Scale*, 2022, learning.oreilly.com/library/view/data-mesh/9781492092384/ [accessed 17 November 2023]

Devlin, B., *Business unIntelligence: Insight and Innovation Beyond Analytics and Big Data*, 2013, Technics Publications, NJ, bit.ly/BunI-TP2 [accessed 14 August 2023]

Engle, J., "Strategies for supporting near real time analytics, OLAP, and interactive data exploration", 2017, www.slideshare.net/awschicago/jeremy-engles-slides-from-redshift-big-data-meetup-on-july-13-2017 [accessed 21 October 2023]

Evans, E., *Domain-Driven Design: Tackling Complexity in the Heart of Software*, 2003, Addison-Wesley, NJ, www.pearson.com/en-us/subject-catalog/p/domain-driven-design-tackling complexity-in-the-heart-of-software/P200000009375/9780321125217 [accessed 18 November 2023]

Evans, E., *Domain-Driven Design Reference: Definitions and Pattern Summaries*, 2015, Domain Language, Inc., www.domainlanguage.com/ddd/reference/ [accessed 18 November 2023]

Frisendal, T., "Handling Data Concerns in 2024 and Onwards", 2024, Dataversity, www.dataversity.net/handling-data-concerns-in-2024-and-onwards/ [accessed 11 February 2024]

Ghosh, P., "The Data Fabric: An Innovative Data Management Solution", 2019, Dataversity, www.dataversity.net/the-data-fabric-an-innovative-data-management-solution/ [accessed 31 October 2023]

Gigerenzer, G., *Gut Feelings: The Intelligence of the Unconscious*, 2007, Penguin Random House, NY, www.penguinrandomhouse.com/books/298863/gut-feelings-by-gerd-gigerenzer/ [accessed 3 August 2023]

Harford, T., *The Logic of Life*, 2008, Random House, NY, timharford.com/books/logicoflife/ [accessed 2 August 2023]

Harvard Business Review, "The New Decision Makers: Equipping Frontline Workers for Success, 2020, HBR Analytic Services and ThoughtSpot, media.thoughtspot.com/pdf/ HBR-ThoughtSpot-The-New-Decision-Makers.pdf [accessed 2 August 2023]

Helland, P., "Data on the Outside versus Data on the Inside", 2005, Proceedings of the 2005 CIDR Conference, www.cidrdb.org/cidr2005/papers/P12.pdf [accessed 26 November 2023]

Heintz, B. & Lee, D., "Productionizing Machine Learning with Delta Lake", 2019, Databricks, www.databricks.com/blog/2019/08/14/productionizing-machine-learning-with-delta-lake.html [accessed 15 August 2023]

Hyperight, "Is Data Mesh right for your organisation?", 2021, hyperight.com/is-data-mesh-right-for-your-organisation/ [accessed 31 December 2023]

IBM, "What is a data fabric?", 2023, IBM, www.ibm.com/topics/data-fabric [accessed 4 November 2023]

IDMA and Devlin, B., *Approaches to Data Design, Engineering, and Development*, 2023 planned, IDMA 203 Course Textbook, Technics Publications, NJ [Not yet published]

Inmon, B. & Srivastava, R., *The Data Lakehouse Architecture*, 2022, Technics Publications, NJ, technicspub.com/data-lakehouse-collection/ [accessed 24 October 2023]

Inmon, B. & Srivastava, R., *Rise of the Data Lakehouse*, 2023, Technics Publications, NJ, technicspub.com/data-lakehouse-collection/ [accessed 24 October 2023]

Jones, M., "Bullshit at the Data Lakehouse", 2020, Good Strategy, goodstrat.com/2020/04/15/bullshit-at-the-data-lakehouse [accessed 24 October 2023]

Jones, M. & Silberzahn, P., "Without An Opinion, You're Just Another Person With Data", 2016, Forbes, www.forbes.com/sites/silberzahnjones/2016/03/15/without-an-opinion-youre-just-another-person-with-data/ [accessed 23 March 2024]

Kahneman, D., *Thinking, Fast and Slow*, 2011, Farrar, Straus and Giroux, NY, us.macmillan.com/books/9781429969352 [accessed 3 August 2023]

Korkrid, A., "Azure Synapse Analytics as a Cloud Lakehouse: A New Data Management Paradigm", 2020, Medium, towardsdatascience.com/azure-synapse-analytics-as-a-cloud-lakehouse-a-new-data-management-paradigm-cdcbe2378209 [accessed 24 October 2023]

L'Esteve, R., "A Cloud Data Lakehouse Success Story", 2022, www.mssqltips.com/sqlservertip/7316/cloud-data-lakehouse-success-story-architecture-outcomes-lessons-learned/ [accessed 16 October 2023]

Lorica, B., Armbrust, M., Xin, R., Zaharia, M., & Ghodsi, A., "What Is a Lakehouse?", 2020, www.databricks.com/blog/2020/01/30/what-is-a-data-lakehouse.html [accessed 6 October 2023]

McKinsey & Company, "Using customer analytics to boost corporate performance", 2014, www.mckinsey.com/capabilities/growth-marketing-and-sales/our-insights/five-facts-how-customer-analytics-boosts-corporate-performance#/ [accessed 2 August 2023]

Merced, A., "Comparison of Data Lake Table Formats (Apache Iceberg, Apache Hudi and Delta Lake)", 2022, www.dremio.com/blog/comparison-of-data-lake-table-formats-apache-iceberg-apache-hudi-and-delta-lake/ [accessed 15 October 2023]

MIT Technology Review Insights, "Laying the foundation for data- and AI-led growth", 2023, www.databricks.com/resources/analyst-papers/laying-foundation-data-and-ai-led-growth [accessed 24 October 2023]

Olinloye, M., "Modern Data Engineering: Building a Data Lakehouse with Apache Spark — Vol 1", DevGenius, blog.devgenius.io/modern-data-engineering-building-a-data-lakehouse-with-apache-spark-vol-1-853f0882862b [accessed 21 October 2023]

O'Neill, C., *Weapons of Math Destruction: How Big Data Increases Inequality and Threatens Democracy*, 2016, Penguin Random House, NY, www.penguinrandomhouse.com/books/241363/weapons-of-math-destruction-by-cathy-oneil/ [accessed 11 August 2023]

Panetta, K., "Gartner Top 10 Data and Analytics Trends for 2021", Gartner, www.gartner.com/smarterwithgartner/gartner-top-10-data-and-analytics-trends-for-2021 [accessed 31 October 2023]

Patnaik, A., "Demystifying Data Fabric Architecture: A Comprehensive Overview", 2023, DZone, dzone.com/articles/demystifying-data-fabric-architecture-a-comprehens [accessed 4 November 2023]

Rosenbaum, A., "Hype Cycle for Data Management, 2023", Gartner, www.gartner.com/en/documents/4573399 [accessed 15 December 2023]

Serra, J., "Data Lakehouse defined", 2021, Blog, //www.jamesserra.com/archive/2021/01/data-lakehouse-defined/ [accessed 24 August 2023]

Strengholt, P., "The Extinction of Enterprise Data Warehousing", 2020, Medium, piethein.medium.com/the-extinction-of-enterprise-data-warehousing-570b0034f47f [accessed 8 September 2023]

Stopford, B., "The Data Dichotomy: Rethinking the Way We Treat Data and Services", 2016, Confluent, www.confluent.io/blog/data-dichotomy-rethinking-the-way-we-treat-data-and-services/ [accessed 25 November 2023]

Walter, B., Ali, A., & Wojtyczka, M., "6 Guiding Principles to Build an Effective Data Lakehouse", 2022, Databricks Blog, www.databricks.com/blog/2022/07/14/6-guiding-principles-to-build-an-effective-data-lakehouse.html [accessed 22 October 2023]

Wikipedia contributors, "List of cognitive biases", 2023, Wikipedia, The Free Encyclopedia, en.wikipedia.org/w/index.php?title= List_of_cognitive_biases [accessed 2 August 2023]

Wynne-Jones, L., "Active Metadata: What It Is, And Why It Matters", Forbes, www.forbes.com/sites/forbestechcouncil/ 2022/06/23/active-metadata-what-it-is-and-why-it-matters/ [accessed 4 November 2023]

Yuhanna, N., "The Forrester Wave™: Big Data Fabric, Q4 2016", 2016, Forrester, www.forrester.com/report/the-forrester-wave-big-data-fabric-q4-2016/RES132141 [accessed 31 October 2023]

Yuhanna, N., "The Forrester Wave™: Enterprise Data Fabric, Q2 2020", www.forrester.com/report/the-forrester-wave-enterprise-data-fabric-q2-2020/RES157288 [accessed 31 October 2023]

Glossary of acronyms

Acronym	Expansion
ACID	Atomicity, consistency, isolation, and durability
ADP	Architectural design pattern
AI	Artificial intelligence
AIM	Action Inputs Model
BI	Business intelligence
CRM	Customer relationship management
CSI	Context-setting information
CSV	Comma-separated variable (file format)
DDD	Domain-driven design (Eric Evans)
DIKW	Data, Information, Knowledge, Wisdom (Russell K. Ackoff)
DLC	Data lake classic ADP
DWC	Data warehouse classic ADP

DWC/cn	Data warehouse classic / cloud native ADP
DWC/op	Data warehouse classic / on premises ADP
EBoC	Enterprise Boundary of Concern
EA	Enterprise architecture
EDM	Enterprise data model
EDW	Enterprise data warehouse
EII	Enterprise information integration
ELT	Extract, Load, and Transform
ETL	Extract, Transform, and Load
ERP	Enterprise resource planning
HSI	Human-sourced information
IDEAL	Integrated, distributed, emergent, adaptive, and latent conceptual architecture
ID	Identifier
IT	Information technology
LDW	Logical data warehouse
M^3	Manifest meaning model

MGD	Machine-generated data
ML	Machine learning
NoSQL	Not only SQL
ORC	Optimized row columnar (file format)
PMD	Process-mediated data
RDBMS	Relational database management system
REAL	Realistic, extensible, actionable, and labile logical architecture
S3	Simple storage service (object store)
SaaS	Software as a service
SOA	Service-oriented architecture
SQL	Structured query language
SSOT	Single source of truth
SVOT	Single version of the truth
W3C	World wide web consortium

INDEX

Page numbers in **bold** indicate definitions or key discussions.

www.ingramcontent.com/pod-product-compliance
Lightning Source LLC
Chambersburg PA
CBHW071239050326
40690CB00011B/2187